NATIONAL DEFENSE RESEARCH

T0288556

Trends in the Draw of Americans to Foreign Terrorist Organizations from 9/11 to Today

Heather J. Williams, Nathan Chandler, Eric Robinson

Prepared for the Office of the Secretary of Defense

For more information on this publication, visit www.rand.org/t/RR2545

Library of Congress Cataloging-in-Publication Data is available for this publication.
ISBN: 978-1-9774-0133-5

Published by the RAND Corporation, Santa Monica, Calif.
© Copyright 2018 RAND Corporation
RAND® is a registered trademark.

Cover Design by Tanya Maiboroda.
Cover Images: Flag: imagesbybarbara/E+/Getty Images.
Faces: Top row left: 101dalmations/E+/Getty Images; Top row right: ncognet0/E+/Getty Images;
Bottom row: Jasmin Merdan/Moment/Getty Images.

Support RAND

Make a tax-deductible charitable contribution at
www.rand.org/giving/contribute

www.rand.org

Preface

This research report analyzes patterns of U.S. persons connected to foreign terrorist organizations (FTOs). The work is intended to enhance understanding regarding the types of individuals drawn to al Qaeda, the Islamic State of Iraq and the Levant (ISIL), and other Islamic terrorist groups. Despite the fact that the overall population of individuals connected to FTOs in the United States is still relatively small, the number of individuals arrested in connection with FTOs rose dramatically after the founding of ISIL. An accurate understanding of the demographic profiles of persons drawn to these groups—and how it has changed over time—may assist counterterrorism efforts. This work is intended to benefit those seeking to understand terrorism within the United States, and particularly those involved in law enforcement and intelligence operations combating terrorism and preventative measures such as countering violent extremism programs.

This research was sponsored by the Office of the Secretary of Defense and conducted within the International Security and Defense Policy Center of the RAND National Defense Research Institute, a federally funded research and development center sponsored by the Office of the Secretary of Defense, the Joint Staff, the Unified Combatant Commands, the U.S. Navy, the U.S. Marine Corps, the defense agencies, and the defense intelligence community.

For more information on the RAND International Security and Defense Policy Center, see www.rand.org/nsrd/ndri/centers/isdp or contact the director (contact information is provided on the webpage).

Contents

Figures and Tables

Summary

The United States witnessed a dramatic increase in domestic arrests connected to foreign terrorist organizations (FTOs) in the wake of the emergence of the Islamic State of Iraq and the Levant (ISIL).[1] Why was ISIL so much more successful than its predecessor, al Qaeda, in recruiting individuals within the United States? Did ISIL appeal to a different segment of the population, or did it make its pitch more effectively than al Qaeda? This report takes a data-driven approach to look at the demographic profile of all publicly known individuals within the United States who have been connected to Islamist FTOs. Whereas previous research has typically examined a segment of data, we have sought to take an expansive approach of all cases in the 16 years following 9/11, regardless of what roles the individual played in relation to an organization—be it direct terrorist operative, homegrown violent extremist, foreign fighter, financier, and/or facilitator.[2] Additionally, we use a transparent and structured approach to determine who should be included and excluded in our analysis to ensure that our data are comprehensive while also excepting cases in which a connection to terrorism is extremely tenuous.

Our analysis has found that ISIL has successfully appealed to a different demographic than al Qaeda, which may be a contributing factor to ISIL's overall greater appeal. ISIL's demographic is not only younger and less educated but has also struck closer to home. Whereas individuals recruited by al Qaeda were more likely to be of Middle Eastern descent and to have immigrated to the United States, those recruited by ISIL were more likely to be U.S. born and African American/black, Caucasian/white, or Latino. For example, for the years 2014–2016, the combined African American and Caucasian population made up 79 percent, 57 percent, and 62 percent of cases annually. Recruits are also increasingly likely to convert to Islam as part of the radicalization process rather than be born or raised Muslim, and are increasingly likely to be female.

---

[1] Alexia Fernandez Campbell, "Why ISIS Recruiting in America Reached Historic Levels," *Atlantic*, December 6, 2015.

[2] We collected data from September 2001 to September 2017.

Our analytic approach also allows us to identify overall trends of foreign terrorism within the United States. Overwhelmingly, most individuals connected to U.S. jihadist terrorism since 9/11 have been U.S. citizens. Of the 476 individuals we have identified, 209 (44 percent) were born in the United States. An additional 129 were born abroad and became naturalized U.S. citizens, and 18 others were U.S. citizens of unknown status (an additional 31 percent, for a combined 75 percent).[3] Of the 26 individuals responsible for the 23 domestic attacks in the United States between September 2001 and September 2017, only two were nonresidents, both of whom entered the country legally; by contrast, 13 were U.S.-born citizens, seven were naturalized U.S. citizens, and four were U.S. legal permanent residents.

Our analysis of the demographic profile of U.S. persons drawn to Islamist terrorism since the rise of ISIL may not match the mental image held by law enforcement, policymakers, and the general public. This creates the potential for a bias in how terrorism prevention and counterterrorism efforts are oriented. The changing racial and national demographic of terrorist recruits suggests that the draw of extremism does not necessarily appeal to something unique among the Muslim or Middle Eastern communities. Instead, the call to extremism—now much more accessible outside those communities, thanks to FTOs' use of social media—appeals to a number of individuals from a variety of backgrounds, albeit a small number. A careful look at many of the cases in this data set show a weak connection of the perpetrator to the FTO and its political goals, and in many cases there was suspected mental illness.

Thankfully, the number of FTO-related arrests and attacks within the United States is still exceedingly small. Spikes in activity (in 2009 and 2015) are deeply alarming to the public, but have not proven to indicate lasting trends. A total of 101 civilians have been killed in the 25 operationalized attacks in the United States between 9/11 and December 31, 2017, and 60 percent of those attacks resulted in no fatalities. Although the terrorism threat is persistent and real, the chances of an American being directly harmed in a terrorist attack is still extremely small. Regardless of those odds, the threat of FTOs to America is potent for the American psyche, and it drives national, state, and local policy in a number of areas. Given that impact, it is important to recognize that the threat from foreign terrorism very often has domestic roots.

---

[3]   To put this figure in perspective, on average an estimated 688,000 people are naturalized in the United States every year. In the 16 years since 9/11, therefore, about 11 million new citizens have been naturalized. See U.S. Citizenship and Immigration Services, "Naturalization Fact Sheet," updated May 19, 2017.

Acknowledgments

The authors would like to thank Rich Girven, Seth Jones, Mike McNerney, and Andrew Parasiliti, whose support has made it possible to undertake this research. Further thanks are due to Colin Clarke and Patrick Johnston for their thorough and constructive comments in quality assurance review, and to Brian Michael Jenkins for comparing notes with us on his concurrent research effort on the origin of homegrown jihadists. We also owe a great debt of gratitude to Charles Kurzman at the University of North Carolina at Chapel Hill for his own diligent collection of relevant data on this subject, and for our helpful conversations about methodology and data sources.

Abbreviations

AFF	aspiring foreign fighter
AIAI	al-Ittihad al-Islami
AQ	al Qaeda
AQAP	al Qaeda in the Arabian Peninsula
AQI	al Qaeda in Iraq
ASG	Abu Sayyaf Group
CVE	countering violent extremism
DOJ	Department of Justice
DTO	direct terrorist operative
FBI	Federal Bureau of Investigation
FF	foreign fighter
FTO	foreign terrorist organization
HIG	Hezb-e-Islami Gulbuddin
HVE	homegrown violent extremists
IG	Islamic Group
IJU	Islamic Jihad Union
IMU	Islamic Movement of Uzbekistan
ISIL	Islamic State of Iraq and the Levant
JeM	Jaish-e-Mohammed
JI	Jemaah Islamiyah
JIS	Jamiyyat Ul-Islam Is-Saheeh
KCF	Khalistan Commando Force
LeT	Lashkar-e-Taiba
LPR	lawful permanent resident
PIJ	Palestinian Islamic Jihad
TTP	Tehrik-e-Taliban Pakistan

CHAPTER ONE

Introduction

The United States witnessed a dramatic increase in domestic arrests connected to foreign terrorist organizations (FTOs) in the wake of the emergence of the Islamic State of Iraq and the Levant (ISIL).[1] Despite the fact that the overall population of individuals connected to FTOs in the United States is still relatively small, the trend seizes public attention, and it raises questions about the relative success of ISIL in attracting individuals within the United States compared to its predecessor organization, al Qaeda. Is ISIL more skillful and adaptive than al Qaeda at recruiting? Has ISIL appealed to a different segment of the population than that touched by al Qaeda? Has ISIL simply displaced al Qaeda as the most infectious voice reaching American audiences who are vulnerable to radicalization, and has this trend continued since ISIL's founding in 2013? This research report seeks to use a structured, methodological approach to identify demographic consistencies or aberrations among these individuals to help answer these questions.

A growing body of scholarship has looked at similar questions; however, much of this work has considered only a portion of this population. For example, some work has looked only at arrests connected to ISIL; other work has looked only at the trends related to foreign fighters; still other work has looked only at plots and attacks executed in the homeland.[2] This study seeks to redress this gap in the academic literature by taking a more expansive approach. More specifically, it analyzes all known cases of U.S. citizens or persons within the United States connected to an FTO with an Islamist jihadist orientation since September 11, 2001. We focus on organizations with an Islamist orientation because these not only represent the majority of U.S. designated

---

[1] Campbell, 2015.

[2] See, for instance, Lorenzo Vidino and Seamus Hughes, "ISIS in America: From Retweets to Raqqa," Washington, D.C.: George Washington University Program on Extremism, December 2015; Peter Bergen, Courtney Schuster, and David Sterman, *ISIS in the West: The New Faces of Extremism*, Washington, D.C.: New America, November 2015; Brian Michael Jenkins, *Inspiration, Not Infiltration: Jihadist Conspirators in the United States*, Santa Monica, Calif.: RAND Corporation, CT-447, December 2015; Thomas Hegghammer, "The Rise of Muslim Foreign Fighters: Islam and the Globalization of Jihad," *International Security*, Vol. 35, No. 3, Winter 2010–2011, pp. 53–94.

FTOs—48 of 64, or 75 percent—but also represent the gross majority of the orientation of those arrested. Although our data set includes any Islamist groups or someone who professes a general cause of jihad, an Islamist orientation also typically means Sunni Islam, with all but three of those groups having a Sunni orientation.[3] For simplicity's sake, we refer to those individuals associated with these FTOs as *jihadist terrorists* in this work. A significant part of this effort was thus spent on defining the appropriate population and identifying the data set, using consistent criteria for including or excluding individuals connected to foreign terrorism. In the sections that follow, we first describe the methodology used to construct and code the universe of cases meriting inclusion in the present inquiry. We then present the quantitative findings of the study. Finally, we conclude by drawing from these results a set of policy implications relevant to U.S. defense, intelligence, and law enforcement agencies, as well as civilian academic and policymaking audiences.

Methodology

Our intent in this study is to examine U.S. cases of foreign terrorism—including foreign fighters (FFs) and homegrown violent extremists (HVEs)—in the post-9/11 environment. Although this would seem a fairly straightforward exercise, determining with methodological rigor which cases should be included in such a data set quickly becomes difficult. In particular, we encountered two major methodological challenges regarding existing resources. First, our research revealed that the majority of existing unclassified data sets on domestic-related terrorists suffer from one or more significant flaws.[4] They often lack transparency about their parameters for case inclusion; they are incomplete and/or not up to date in their coverage; they draw coding details from nonscholarly or unofficial secondary sources, such as internet blogs or chat forums, non–peer reviewed "academic" publications, or biased news media outlets; they circumscribe their case universe to a narrow set of individuals, such as only those who have carried out or attempted to carry out an attack or who are inspired or associated with ISIL. Some include, in their case universe, individuals whose goals and ideologies are beyond the scope of this study, such as extreme right-wing nationalists or left-wing environmental terrorists.

Second, in constructing our case universe, relying on public information about arrests or indictments of individuals is methodologically problematic. Many terrorism-

---

[3]   The three groups that are not Sunni oriented are Lebanese Hezbollah and Kata'ib Hezbollah, which are both Shi'a oriented, and the Iraqi-based Jaysh Rijal al-Tariq al-Naqshbandi (aka the Naqshbandi Army), which is a militant Sufi organization. (Although, notably, none of our cases was associated with the Naqshbandi Army.)

[4]   As is discussed in more detail in the following section, one notable exception is Charles Kurzman's research on Muslim American involvement with violent extremism.

related cases at least start with sealed indictments, meaning that our case universe is likely not complete. The National Security Division within the U.S. Department of Justice (DOJ) issues press releases for cases with a connection to international terrorism, but its online history only goes back to 2009. Moreover, the issuance of press releases on more recent cases is often slowed because of connections between ongoing investigations. Relatedly, while DOJ and other open-source data are relatively reliable regarding cases of individuals who have been arrested in the act of attempting to travel abroad to join an FTO, unclassified information on U.S. persons who have successfully journeyed to a foreign battlefield is far less transparent.[5] Therefore, our data may risk bias by excluding less-known or unknown historic cases. Furthermore, it should be recognized that terrorism arrests are only made when law enforcement agents are confident that they have enough evidence to obtain a conviction; in the absence of the standard of proof necessary to convict on terrorism-related charges, authorities may instead arrest a would-be terrorist on simpler criminal charges such as immigration violations.[6] Although we included cases where the Federal Bureau of Investigation (FBI) or other government agency documents identified the arrest as being in connection to a terrorist investigation (unless no connection to terrorism was ever discovered), this tendency may introduce an additional underreporting bias to our data set.[7] On the other hand, changes in the focus or aggressiveness of law enforcement, or changes in its legal authority to pursue certain cases, may artificially skew the population of U.S. persons arrested on terrorism-related charges in the other direction. As FBI counterterrorism sting operations and informant networks have proliferated in the post-9/11 era, for instance, the bureau has regularly been criticized by outside observers as "leading" relatively innocuous threats—essentially loudmouths and jihadist "wannabes"—down a path toward terrorist activity that they might not otherwise take.[8] We did not exam-

---

[5] For instance, at the peak of ISIL's territorial control in 2015, various sources estimated the number of Americans who had successfully traveled to Iraq and Syria to join Sunni militant organizations as between 100 and 150—up from only a couple dozen in late 2013. Our data set, however, identifies by name only a fraction of this total estimated number of U.S. FFs. See Peter Neumann, "Foreign Fighter Total in Syria/Iraq Now Exceeds 20,000; Surpasses Afghanistan Conflict in the 1980s," International Centre for the Study of Radicalisation and Political Violence, January 26, 2015; Aaron Zelin, *ICSR Insight: Up to 11,000 Foreign Fighters in Syria, Steep Rise Among Western Europeans*, London: International Centre for the Study of Radicalisation and Political Violence, December 12, 2013; Soufan Group, "Foreign Fighters: An Updated Assessment of the Flow of Foreign Fighters into Syria and Iraq," New York: Soufan Group, December 2015; and Nicholas J. Rasmussen, "Current Terrorist Threat to the United States," hearing before the Senate Select Committee on Intelligence, February 12, 2015.

[6] John Mueller and Mark G. Stewart, "The Terrorism Delusion: America's Overwrought Response to September 11," *International Security*, Vol. 37, No. 1, Summer 2012, p. 94.

[7] Indeed, according to one FBI estimate, just one in four terrorism cases actually result in terrorism-related charges. Garrett Graff, *The Threat Matrix: The FBI at War in the Age of Terror*, New York: Little, Brown, and Company, 2011, p. 557.

[8] These trends seem to have accelerated in the post-ISIL era. By one recent account, "Undercover Operations, once seen as a last resort, are now used in about two of every three prosecutions involving people suspected of

ine whether the tactics used by the FBI in its investigations had changed in relation to this criticism or by other factors, or whether there are differences between regions and jurisdictions. Trends of this nature on the part of law enforcement might thus create problems in truly understanding the draw of U.S. persons to foreign terrorism based on an examination of the population of individuals arrested on terrorism-related charges. Finally, as we note in greater detail in the following pages, coding certain biographical variables of interest on would-be terrorists—such as highest level of education, history of conversion to Islam, race/ethnicity, and the like—based on information available in the public record is methodologically challenging; in some cases, these data points could not be obtained.[9] We have attempted in our findings to be as transparent as possible about these limitations.

Ultimately, we defined the population of interest as meeting one of six mutually exclusive criteria. These criteria serve to scope the population geographically to individuals closely tied to the United States; most thus meet the governmental definition of "U.S. persons"—U.S.-born citizens, U.S. naturalized citizens, and lawful permanent residents (LPRs). Our criteria also serve to scope the population legally to individuals closely associated with or inspired by officially designated FTOs with Islamist orientations. The criteria thus relate to the key federal statutes on providing or attempting to provide material support to terrorist organizations, particularly under 18 U.S. Code, Sections 2339A and 2339B.

The first criterion for inclusion was any U.S. persons arrested inside the United States on terrorism-related charges in connection with a designated FTO and/or espousing Islamist ideologies.[10] The second part of this parameter was intended to exclude, for instance, persons who were ideologically motivated by extreme right- or left-wing agendas, terroristic incidents of workplace violence or hate crimes, as well as high-profile

---

supporting the Islamic State, a sharp rise in the span of just two years"; Eric Lichtblau, "F.B.I. Steps Up Use of Stings in ISIS Cases," *New York Times*, June 7, 2016. See also Jesse J. Norris and Hanna Grol-Prokopczyk, "Estimating the Prevalence of Entrapment in Post-9/11 Terrorism Cases," *Journal of Criminal Law and Criminology*, Vol. 105, No. 3, 2015, pp. 609–678; Trevor Aaronson, "The Informants: The FBI Has Built a Massive Network of Spies to Prevent Another Domestic Attack. But Are They Busting Terrorist Plots—Or leading Them?" *Mother Jones*, September–October 2011; Human Rights Watch, *Illusion of Justice: Human Rights Abuses in US Terrorism Prosecutions*, New York: Human Rights Watch, 2014; Caroline Simon, "The FBI Is 'Manufacturing Terrorism Cases' on a Greater Scale Than Ever Before," *Business Insider*, June 9, 2016; and Heather Maher, "How the FBI Helps Terrorists Succeed," *Atlantic*, February 26, 2013.

[9] We have relied generally on observer-reported or legal data to identify race, which may be inaccurate in some cases. We made our race categories mutually exclusive, which affected seven cases of individuals of mixed Middle Eastern/South Asian and Caucasian/white descent, which we coded as Middle Eastern/South Asian. It also affected two cases of individuals of mixed African American/black and Caucasian/white descent, the brothers Ahmed and Muhammed Bilal, which we coded as African American/black, as they were identified in legal documents.

[10] For the current list of FTOs as designated by the U.S. Secretary of State under Section 219 of the Immigration and Nationality Act, see U.S. Department of State, "Foreign Terrorist Organizations," undated.

terrorist attacks unassociated with an FTO, such as the post-9/11 anthrax attacks and the 2002 Washington, D.C., Beltway snipers. It was also intended to exclude U.S. persons associated with non-Islamist FTOs, such as the Revolutionary Armed Forces of Colombia or the Real Irish Republican Army. The second criterion was non-U.S. persons arrested inside the United States in connection with a designated FTO and for crimes that they intended to commit inside the United States. This, for example, could include individuals on temporary visas to the United States or individuals illegally in the country. The third criterion was U.S. persons arrested outside the United States in connection with an FTO and extradited to the United States for trial. This definition covers a number of U.S. FFs captured abroad through collaborative efforts with U.S. law enforcement. The fourth criterion was U.S. persons killed overseas while an active member of an FTO, including FFs. The fifth criterion was U.S. persons and non-U.S. persons killed inside the United States while in the process of conducting a terrorist act in the name of an FTO. This parameter could include an individual operating either as a direct foreign agent of an FTO or indirectly inspired by an FTO as a so-called lone wolf. The sixth criterion was U.S. persons currently known to be outside the United States who have an outstanding warrant for arrest in relation to an FTO, or who remain at large as FFs as publicly acknowledged by U.S. intelligence and law enforcement sources. Of course, as noted above, there are likely many more instances of unknowable, sealed indictments related to wanted FFs.

We also applied five explicit criteria for exclusion from the data set. The first criterion was non-U.S. persons arrested outside the United States in connection with an FTO who were subsequently extradited to the United States for trial or for detention under an illegal combatant status, such as the detainees at Guantanamo Bay. This could include individuals accused of attacking U.S. interests abroad, such as a U.S. embassy, or attempting to conduct a terrorist plot within the United States; such cases do not, however, inform the discussion of the draw of Americans to foreign terrorism. The second criterion was non-U.S. persons arrested while in the United States while attempting to leave the United States to join an FTO. The third criterion was individuals who had been indicted on terrorism-related charges, but were found innocent or had the charges dropped for reasons such as a hung jury. The fourth criterion was individuals who were found guilty on minor terrorism-related accessory charges not explicitly covered under the key terrorism statutes of U.S. federal law—18 U.S. Code, Sections 2339A or 2339B—and who did not face any jail time. Such examples might include a parent who was found guilty of lying to federal investigators in order to protect his or her child but faced no posttrial sentencing besides jail time served. Finally, we excluded from the case universe individuals indicted or convicted on terrorism-related charges after September 11, 2001, if the alleged crime committed occurred before that day.

Even these relatively precise parameters, however, did not circumscribe all of the cases relevant to our goal of looking at the draw of foreign terrorism to those in the

United States. In a few instances, we were thus required to make exceptions to our own coding rules.[11] An example of this difficulty is the case of Aafia Siddiqui, also known as Lady al Qaeda. Siddiqui is a Pakistani citizen who lived in the United States from 1990 to 2003, during which time she earned a B.S. from the Massachusetts Institute of Technology and a Ph.D. from Brandeis University and gave birth to two children (who therefore are U.S. citizens). Siddiqui was arrested in Afghanistan in 2008 and extradited to the United States, where she is now serving an 86-year sentence. By our own exclusion criteria, Siddiqui—as a non-U.S. citizen arrested outside the United States for crimes committed abroad—should not be included in our data set. However, Siddiqui was almost certainly radicalized while in the United States, and it was this radicalization that prompted her to leave the country in 2002. She is often described as an American despite her official citizenship status. For these reasons we elected to include Siddiqui in our data set.

Similarly, we decided to exclude a number of borderline cases from our data set because we determined that the observation did not have a strong bearing on the central research question—reasons and trends of U.S. persons drawn to foreign terrorism—even if the case did not satisfy one of the explicit exclusion criteria described above. For instance, in a number of financial criminal cases, individuals indicted on fraud or drug trafficking conspiracies were secondarily arraigned of terrorism-related charges, such as violating the sanctions regime on Iraq or providing donations to an Islamic charity with known or suspected ties to an FTO. In such cases we excluded the individual from our data set based on the justification that the defendant's activities truly resembled that of an organized criminal—not a radicalized U.S. citizen—and that terrorism-related charges were likely added secondarily to strengthen the prosecution's case. As another example of exclusion exceptions, we occasionally omitted from our data set persons who were convicted on terrorism-related charges but who appeared to be only incidental accessories to a terrorist-related crime and exhibited no evidence of radicalization. For instance, we excluded the cases of Robel Kidane Phillipos and Azamat Tazhayakov, friends of Dzhokhar Tsarnaev who were convicted of obstruction of justice and tampering with evidence in the wake of the Boston Marathon bombings in 2013 after they destroyed property belonging to Tsarnaev and lied to federal investigators.

In sum, in compiling the case universe for this study, we have endeavored to err on the side of inclusion—but within limits. Our purpose is not to analyze every individual indicted on any terrorism related-charge in the United States since 9/11. Rather, it is to focus our observations on the population of U.S. citizens and non-U.S. citizens residing in the country who have exhibited a strong draw toward foreign terrorism and a disposition toward Islamic radicalization. In so doing we have attempted to improve

---

[11] These exceptions constitute less than 1 percent of the 476 observations in the case universe population.

upon existing data sets by balancing the goal of comprehensiveness with a standard of rigorous coding transparency.

Data Sources

After these parameters were established for the terrorist data set, we performed research to identify individuals who met the inclusion criteria. This necessitated consulting multiple data sets of varying degrees of inclusiveness. Two sources, in particular, were found to be exceptionally comprehensive: the data set for University of North Carolina sociologist Charles Kurzman's *Muslim American Involvement with Violent Extremism, 2016* and DOJ's list of public, unsealed terrorism and terrorism-related convictions since September 11, 2001.[12] While these sources provided a strong foundation for the universe of cases satisfying our criteria of inquiry, they did not fully complete it. For instance, they included neither recent indictments nor instances of U.S. citizens who had traveled abroad to become FFs but against whom charges were never filed. Additionally, many individuals included in these lists violated our exclusion parameters. Moreover, these resources lacked details on many of the variables we sought to code as part of this investigation. We have also compared data with our RAND colleague Brian Michael Jenkins, who has done concurrent work examining HVEs and their age, citizenship status, religion, and country of origin.[13]

To finalize our case universe—and to complete our case codings—we thus supplemented these lists with numerous other think tank studies, DOJ and FBI press releases, news reports, journal articles, nongovernmental organization data sets, and other official government publications on terrorism statistics.[14] In the vast majority

---

[12] Charles Kurzman, *Muslim-American Involvement with Violent Extremism, 2016*, Durham, N.C.: Triangle Center on Terrorism and Homeland Security, 2016. For Kurzman's most recent data set, see Charles Kurzman, *Muslim-American Involvement with Violent Extremism, 2018*, webpage, undated. See also U.S. Department of Justice, *Hearing Before the Committee on Oversight and Government Reform, United States House of Representatives, Entitled "Seeking Justice for Victims of Palestinian Terrorism in Israel," February 2, 2016*, Washington, D.C.: U.S. Department of Justice, undated.

[13] Michael Jenkins, *The Origin of America's Jihadists*, Santa Monica, Calif.: RAND Corporation, PE-251-RC, December 2017.

[14] See, for instance, U.S. House of Representatives, Homeland Security Committee, *Final Report of the Task Force on Combatting Terrorist and Foreign Fighter Travel*, Washington, D.C., March 2015; U.S. House of Representatives, Homeland Security Committee, "Terrorist Threat Snapshot: Homegrown Jihadist Cases Since 9/11," webpage, undated; Jessica Zuckerman, Steven Bucci, and James Jay Carafano, "60 Terrorist Plots Since 9/11: Continued Lessons in Domestic Counterterrorism," Special Report #137 on Terrorism, Washington, D.C.: Heritage Foundation, July 22, 2013; Bergen, Schuster, and Sterman, 2015; Riley Walters, "An Interactive Timeline of the 85 Islamist Terror Plots Since 9/11," *Daily Signal*, May 16, 2016; Counter Extremism Project, "Terrorists and Extremists Database," webpage, undated; Brian Michael Jenkins, *Stray Dogs and Virtual Armies: Radicalization and Recruitment to Jihadist Terrorism in the United States Since 9/11*, Santa Monica, Calif.: RAND Corporation, OP-343-RC, 2011; Jenkins, 2015; National Consortium for the Study of Terrorism and Responses to Terrorism,

of cases, our codings were also informed by publicly available criminal complaints, indictments, statements of facts, and/or plea agreements.[15]

Data Fields

The terrorist data set contains 476 individuals coded along approximately three dozen dimensions. These variables include details on perpetrator demographics (e.g., age, race/ethnicity, geographic location, education level, etc.); terrorist history (e.g., terrorist role, plot description, FTO associations and contacts, history of conversion to Islam, etc.); and experience in the U.S. criminal justice system (e.g., charges filed, statutes convicted under, plea arrangements, sentencing verdicts, etc.). In the Appendix to this report, Table A.1 lists and defines each of these fields further; Table A.2 details the population of individuals studied and includes the codings of several key biographical data fields for these 476 persons. As discussed in more detail in the subsequent section on our statistical findings, it should be noted that in some cases, open-source biographical information was not available, and thus not every variable could be coded for every individual included in the data set.

"Global Terrorism Database," webpage, undated; Yousef Taha, "Memorandum: ISIS-Related Prosecutions in the United States Through July 29, 2015," Rochester: Federal Public Defender's Office for the Western District of New York, July 29, 2015; U.S. Federal Bureau of Investigation, "Ten Years After: The FBI Since 9/11. Investigative Highlights: Major Terrorism Preventions, Disruptions, and Investigations," press release, Washington, D.C.: U.S. Federal Bureau of Investigation, 2011; Hegghammer, 2010–2011; John Mueller, ed., *Terrorism Since 9/11: The American Cases*, Washington, D.C.: Cato Institute, March 2016; Anti-Defamation League, "Homegrown Islamic Extremism in 2014," April, 2015; Center on Law and Security, *Terrorist Trial Report Card: September 11, 2001–September 11, 2011*, New York: Center on Law and Security, New York University School of Law, January 2010; U.S. Department of Justice, *The Accomplishments of the U.S. Department of Justice, 2001–2009*, Washington, D.C.: U.S. Department of Justice, March 8, 2010; Richard Zabel and James Benjamin, Jr., *In Pursuit of Justice: Prosecuting Terrorism Cases in the Federal Courts*, New York: Human Rights First, May 2008; Robin Simcox and Emily Dyer, *Al-Qaeda in the United States: A Complete Analysis of Terrorism Offenses*, London: Henry Jackson Society, 2013; Peter Bergen, "Post-9/11 Jihadist Terrorism Cases Involving U.S. Citizens and Residents: An Overview," March 13, 2011; Robin Simcox, "'We Will Conquer Your Rome': A Study of Islamic Terror Plots in the West," Henry Jackson Society, September 29, 2015; Transactional Records Access Clearinghouse, Syracuse University, "TRAC Reports on Terrorism," webpage, undated; Erik J. Dahl, "The Plots that Failed: Intelligence Lessons Learned from Unsuccessful Terrorist Attacks Against the United States," *Studies in Conflict & Terrorism*, Vol. 34, No. 8, 2011, pp. 621–648.

[15] One of the best centralized repositories for these legal documents is the Investigative Project on Terrorism, which maintains a database regarding individuals indicted on terrorism and/or terrorism-related charges; Investigative Project on Terrorism, "Court Cases," webpage, undated.

Data Grouping

In the findings that follow, we first briefly present statistical trends in domestic terrorism-related arrests and radicalization irrespective of specific FTO associations, followed by a more refined analysis examining the differences broken down by three organizational groupings: ISIL, al Qaeda and its formal affiliates[16] (excluding al Shabaab), and "other groups." FTOs included in the data set's "other groups" are Abu Sayyaf Group, al-Gamaa al-Islamiyya (aka Islamic Group), Chechen Mujahideen, Hamas, Hezb-e-Islami Gulbuddin, Iran's Qods Force, Islamic Jihad Union, Islamic Movement of Uzbekistan, Jaish-e-Mohammed, Jemaah Islamiyah, Khalistan Commando Force, LeT, Lebanese Hezbollah, Palestinian Islamic Jihad, the Afghan Taliban, and Tehrik-e-Taliban Pakistan. Three methodological caveats should be noted regarding group codings.

First, while Somalia's al Shabaab remains today a formal affiliate of al Qaeda, the decision to treat it distinctly from the other al Qaeda affiliates was informed primarily by the observation that 31 of the 37 individuals in the data set directly associated with al Shabaab established connections with the group before it had officially become an al Qaeda–associated group in 2012.[17] Additionally, as discussed in greater detail in Chapter Two (see Box 2.1), the interaction between the American Somali diaspora and FTOs was discovered to highlight several broader trends that emerge from the data comparing the pre- and post-ISIL eras.[18]

---

[16] In addition to core al Qaeda—whose top leadership is believed by most Western intelligence sources to be hiding in Pakistan—this analytical grouping includes the official affiliates of al Qaeda in the Arabian Peninsula (AQAP), al Qaeda in the Islamic Maghreb, al Qaeda in the Indian Subcontinent, and Jabhat Fath al-Sham (formerly known as Jabhat al-Nusra). It also includes individuals who identified with the affiliate al Qaeda in Iraq (AQI), the predecessor organization of ISIL, prior to the latter's splintering from the former in 2013. For analyses on the evolution of the al Qaeda–ISIS split, see Clint Watts, "ISIS and al Qaeda Race to the Bottom: The Next Attacks," *Foreign Affairs*, November 23, 2015; Mary Habeck, "Assessing the ISIS–al Qaeda Split," SITE Intelligence Group, July 2014; and Seth G. Jones, James Dobbins, Daniel Byman, Christopher Chivvis, Ben Connable, Jeffrey Martini, Eric Robinson, and Nathan Chandler, *Rolling Back the Islamic State*, Santa Monica, Calif.: RAND, RR-1912, 2017, Chapter Two, "The Rise and Decline of the Islamic State," pp. 13–38.

[17] Of course, it should be noted that at least some subset of these individuals might have joined al Shabaab with the expectation that the group *would become* an al Qaeda affiliate; absent an observable counterfactual, reverse causality cannot be ruled out here.

[18] On trends in the Somali American diaspora in homegrown U.S. terrorist threats and overseas FF populations, see, for instance, Erroll Southers and Justin Heinz, *Foreign Fighters: Terrorist Recruitment and Countering Violent Extremism (CVE) Programs in Minneapolis–St. Paul: A Qualitative Field Study*, Los Angeles: National Center of Excellence for Risk and Economic Analysis of Terrorism Events, April 2015; Scott E. Mulligan, *Radicalization Within the Somali-American Diaspora: Countering the Homegrown Terrorist Threat*, Monterey, Calif.: Naval Postgraduate School, December 2009; Steve Weine and Osman Ahmed, *Building Resilience to Violent Extremism Among Somali-Americans in Minneapolis–St. Paul*, College Park, Md.: National Consortium for the Study of Terrorism and Responses to Terrorism, 2012; Josh Richardson, "The Somali Diaspora: A Key Counterterrorism Ally," *CTC Sentinel*, Vol. 4, No. 7, July 1, 2011, pp. 12–14; and Stephen M. Hill, "Community Policing, Homeland Security, and the Somali Diaspora in Minnesota," *Democracy and Security*, Vol. 13, No. 3, July 17, 2017, pp. 246–266.

Second, in approximately 10 percent of cases examined, evidence suggested that an individual was strongly radicalized by the influence—direct or indirect—of multiple groups. Oftentimes these convergent influences or inspirational sources were FTOs that are formally or informally allied, such as al Qaeda and AQAP or the Afghan Taliban and Lashkar-e-Taiba (LeT). Other times, however, the multiple FTO associations included groups in direct rivalry or conflict with each other, such as Jabhat al-Nusra and ISIL, possibly suggesting the individual's more fluid group identity.[19] Out of analytical necessity, we endeavored in each case to render a qualitative assessment of the earliest and/or strongest FTO influence on an individual's radicalization process in order to assign each person a "primary group." In most cases this could be done with a relatively high degree of confidence, but others proved more challenging. For instance, Ahmad Abousamra was a French-born, naturalized U.S. citizen and Massachusetts resident who is believed to have fled the United States in late 2006 after coming under increased FBI scrutiny in connection with previous trips made between 2002 and 2004 to Iraq, Pakistan, and Yemen to train, presumably in al Qaeda–affiliated military camps. In 2009 he was indicted in absentia in a U.S. federal court for providing material support to an FTO, and in 2015 he was killed in an air strike in Syria, where he had been fighting with ISIL since at least 2013.[20] In this case we coded Abousamra's primary group affiliation as al Qaeda rather than ISIL, since the earliest evidence of his radicalizing influence—our dependent variable of interest—can be placed in 2002. In short, while it is recognized that this coding convention might unavoidably introduce an additional source of bias in the statistical analysis, it is expected that the effect of such bias will not be strong overall given the relatively few number of cases in which the problem presents itself.

Third, in approximately 7 percent of cases examined—nearly all of which were of HVEs—our examination of the related criminal complaints, indictments, DOJ and FBI press releases, and other publicly available government documents and media accounts did not reveal a clear connection between the individual and a specific FTO. Rather, these U.S. persons appeared to have been drawn to extremist activities not

---

[19] As Nicholas Rasmussen, director of the National Counterterrorism Center, recently remarked, "We might be moving into a new era in which centralized leadership of a terrorist organization matters less, group identity is more fluid, and violent extremist narratives focus on a wider range of alleged grievances and enemies"; Rasmussen, 2015. There are, of course, other plausible explanations for U.S. persons being drawn to rival FTOs that are in direct opposition to each other. For instance, underlying divisions between rival terrorist organizations may often be stronger at the strategic levels—where leaders must compete for resources, recruits, and popular support, and where leaders may disagree over nuanced Koranic interpretations and details regarding the operational balance between strategy and tactics (e.g., concerning the acceptability of Shi'a Muslim civilian casualties)—than at the tactical/foot soldier level. For a more in-depth discussion of the apparent "trend in violent lone actors whose ideologies are broadly jihadist, but not tied to any one group," see Paige Pascarelli, "Ideology à la Carte: Why Lone Actor Terrorists Choose and Fuse Ideologies," Lawfare, October 2, 2016.

[20] United States v. Tarek Mehanna and Ahmad Abousamra, U.S. District Court of Massachusetts, Cr. No. 09-CR-10017-GAO.

because of a progressive intensification of Islamist ideology or deepening sense of group identification with a particular FTO but because of the convergence of a multitude of overlapping social, personal, or political risk factors. For example, in June 2011 Abu Khalid Abdul-Latif—a U.S.-born convert to Islam, who in a previous felony criminal proceeding was evaluated as possibly possessing "some psychological issues"— was indicted after an FBI investigation uncovered his plot to bomb a Seattle military recruiting center in retribution for "perceived atrocities committed by the United States Military in the Middle East."[21] While witness testimony and forensic electronic investigations revealed Abdul-Latif's general admiration for Osama bin Laden, Anwar al-Awlaki, and Fort Hood shooter Nidal Hasan, no evidence was ever presented at trial confirming that Abdul-Latif ever directly supported, contacted, swore allegiance to, or intended to act in the name of al Qaeda or any of its affiliates. In such cases as this ($n = 39$), we have coded the individual's group identity as "none ('jihad')" and have analyzed the case among the aforementioned bin for "other groups."

---

[21] United States v. Abu Khalid Abdul-Latif (aka Joseph Anthony Davis) and Walli Mujahidh (aka Frederick Domingue, Jr.), U.S. District Court, Western District of Washington at Seattle, Case No. MJ11-292, amended complaint for violations, June 23, 2011.

CHAPTER TWO

Findings

Key Trends in Radicalization of U.S. Persons Since 9/11

The terrorist threat in the U.S. homeland remains persistent, multidimensional, and in constant evolution.[1] What was once primarily viewed as a security risk emanating from abroad has increasingly become an internal one characterized by HVEs inspired by electronic propaganda and, most recently, by the danger of FFs returning from battlefields in Afghanistan, Iraq, Pakistan, Somalia, Syria, and Yemen. Notwithstanding the relatively few instances of successful domestic terrorist attacks in the decade and a half since 9/11, the rate of attacks has increased since ISIL's emergence, as is shown in Table 2.1. With the exception of the June 2016 massacre in Orlando, Florida, the rate of lethality has remained generally low, with no victim causalities occurring in 60 percent of cases. This section seeks to assess key trends in the population of nearly 500 U.S. persons who between September 2001 and September 2017 have either been arrested for plotting to commit an act of terrorist or for providing material support to an FTO; have been killed while executing a domestic attack or fighting abroad with an FTO; or are publicly known to be at large, fighting in the ranks of an FTO.

In seeking to better understand the draw of U.S. persons to foreign Islamic terrorist organizations, we frequently employ the term *radicalization* to denote the process by which an individual, fed and nurtured by a variety of influences, adopts an extremist religious or political ideology and ultimately embraces the use of violence or terrorist tactics.[2] However, it should be recognized that this term, now widely used in scholarly publications, government documents, and the popular media, is highly debated. While an in-depth review of the many theoretical models describing this typically gradual,

---

[1] Between September 12, 2001, and December 31, 2017, there have been only 25 Islamist jihadi terror attack plots within the U.S. homeland that successfully advanced to the operational phase. These domestic attacks have resulted in 102 victim fatalities and the deaths of 13 perpetrators. In 15 cases (60 percent), no victim casualties occurred. In three cases (those of Umar Abulmutallab, Richard Reid, and Faisal Shahzad), the perpetrators' primitive bombs failed to detonate.

[2] Mitchell Silber and Arvin Bhatt, *Radicalization in the West: The Homegrown Threat*, New York: New York City Police Department, 2007, pp. 16–18.

Table 2.1
Universe of Operationalized Islamist Jihadi Terror Attacks in the U.S. Homeland After 9/11

Perpetrator(s)	Plot Name	Year	Location	Fatalities[a]
Richard Reid	"Shoe bomber" attack	2001	Paris to Miami, Fla., flight	0
Hesham Hadayet*	Los Angeles International Airport shootings	2002	Los Angeles, Calif.	2
Mohammed Taheri-azar	University of North Carolina attack	2006	Chapel Hill, N.C.	0
Carlos Bledsoe	Little Rock shootings	2009	Little Rock, Ark.	1
Nidal Hasan	Fort Hood shootings	2009	Fort Hood, Tex.	13
Umar Abulmutallab	"Underwear bomber" attack	2009	Amsterdam to Detroit, Mich., flight	0
Faisal Shahzad	Times Square bombing	2010	New York, N.Y.	0
Yonathan Melaku	Northern Virginia military facility shootings	2011	Arlington, Chantilly, and Woodbridge, Va.	0
Dzhokhar Tsarnaev, Tamerlan Tsarnaev*	Boston Marathon bombings	2010	Boston and Cambridge, Mass.	5[b]
Zale Thompson*	New York City Police Department hatchet attack	2014	Queens, N.Y.	0
Ali Muhammad Brown	Washington/New Jersey murder spree	2014	Seattle, Wash.; West Orange, N.J.	4
Elton Simpson,* Nadr Soofi*	Garland shootings	2015	Garland, Tex.	0
Usaamah Rahim,*	Boston beheading plot	2015	Boston, Mass.	0
Mohammad Abdulazeez*	Chattanooga shootings	2015	Chattanooga, Tenn.	5
Faisal Mohammad*	University of California, Merced stabbings	2015	Merced, Calif.	0
Syed Farook,* Tashfeen Malik*	San Bernardino attack	2015	San Bernardino, Calif.	14
Munther Saleh	New York Police Department stabbing attack	2015	New York, N.Y.	0
Edward Archer	Philadelphia Police Department attack	2016	Philadelphia, Pa.	0
Omar Mateen*	Pulse Nightclub attack	2016	Orlando, Fla.	49
Dahir Adan*	St. Cloud mall stabbings	2016	St. Cloud, Minn.	0

Perpetrator(s)	Plot Name	Year	Location	Fatalities[a]
Ahmad Rahami	Queens/Northern New Jersey bomb attacks	2016	Queens, N.Y.; Seaside and Elizabeth, N.J.	0
Abdul Artan*	Ohio State University car/knifing attack	2016	Columbus, Ohio	0
Joshua Cummings	Regional Transportation District security guard attack	2017	Denver, Colo.	1
Sayfullo Saipov[c]	New York truck attack	2017	New York, N.Y.	8
Akayed Ullah[c]	Times Square subway bombing	2017	New York, N.Y.	0

[a] Fatality counts exclude perpetrator deaths that occurred during law enforcement's response to the attack.

[b] Uniquely, this figure includes the deaths of two law enforcement officers, Sean Collier and Dennis Simmonds, who died as a result of wounds suffered after the Boston Marathon bombings. Massachusetts Institute of Technology police officer Sean Collier was assassinated during the Tsarnaevs' attempted escape in the days immediately following the bombing; Boston police officer Dennis Simmonds died nearly a year after the bombing from grenade wounds sustained during the concluding hours of the manhunt for the Tsarnaevs. We would also note the high number of injuries from the Boston Marathon bombings, with 264 civilians injured and 16 persons losing one or multiple limbs, according to public reports.

[c] The October 2017 and December 2017 Manhattan attacks conducted by Sayfullo Saipov and Akayed Ullah, respectively, occurred after the conclusion of data collection for this study, which was temporally bounded by the population of individuals who were arrested, were killed, or traveled abroad as FFs between September 12, 2001, and September 30, 2017. The statistical analysis in the following sections of discussion do not, therefore, include these individuals.

* Perpetrators killed during law enforcement's response to attacks.

transformational process is beyond the scope of the present study, it is worth highlighting several major commonalities among those contained in the vast academic literature on this subject.

First, most conceptual paradigms agree that the multistep pathway to violence is caused by a "complex mix of personal, political, and social drivers" involving "multiple push/pull factors"; unfortunately, "very little [is known] about the temporal ordering of risk factors . . . across terrorists."[3] Some frameworks posit that the progression is linear; some do not. As Michael King and Donald Taylor summarize in their comparative analysis of several major theoretical frameworks,

---

[3]   Emily Corner and Paul Gill, "Is There a Nexus Between Terrorist Involvement and Mental Health in the Age of the Islamic State?" *CTC Sentinel*, Vol. 10, No. 1, January 2017, p. 6; Paul Gill and Emily Corner, "There and Back Again: The Study of Mental Disorder and Terrorist Involvement," *American Psychologist*, Vol. 72, No. 3, 2017, pp. 232, 239.

> The models converge on the assumption that radicalization is a transformation based on social-psychological processes . . . [they] describe emotions, cognitions, and social influences that, when operating in the right order and combination, can lead someone to endorse and engage in terrorism.[4]

Second, the various models' first phase typically proceeds from an internalization of factors in the individual's life situation (e.g., socioeconomic status, education, religion, neighborhood, personality, peer and familial relations, personal crises, mental disorders, experiences with discrimination or victimization, etc.) prior to exposure to extremist ideologies. According to many theoretical models, at the beginning of the process an individual typically experiences feelings of personal or group relative deprivation based on subjective or objective perceptions.[5] Randy Borum, for instance, labels this stage "social and economic deprivation"; Fathali Moghaddam identifies it as "psychological interpretation of material conditions"; Marc Sageman, who posits a nonsequential model, describes three interplaying cognitive factors, "a sense of moral outrage," "the frame used to interpret the world," and "resonance with personal experience"; Mitchell Silber and Arvin Bhatt name it "pre-radicalization"; and Quitan Wiktorowicz calls it the "cognitive opening."[6]

Third, though the models show more theoretical variance in the intermediate phases of the radicalization process, they share many common themes. They typically emphasize a progression in which individuals seek out and show a receptiveness to new religious and/or political influences; debate and explore new beliefs while challenging old ones; and begin to form new identities in order to rectify perceived injustices. Later, worldviews may shift further, attitudes harden, and blame of other out-groups increase as individuals continue to socialize with like-minded individuals with shared grievances (either in person or online), demonstrate deference to thought leaders, differentiate and retreat from the mainstream, and channel discontent toward specific targets. Finally, the sequencing may conclude with an individual's full embrace of an extremist ideology, formal adoption of a new group identity, and legitimization of violent tactics.[7]

---

[4]   Michael King and Donald Taylor, "The Radicalization of Homegrown Jihadists: A Review of Theoretical Models and Social Psychological Evidence," *Terrorism and Political Violence,* Vol. 23, No. 4, 2011, p. 609.

[5]   King and Taylor, 2011, pp. 609–610.

[6]   Randy Borum, "Understanding the Terrorist Mindset," *FBI Law Enforcement Bulletin*, Vol. 72, No. 7, July 2003, p. 9; Fathali Moghaddam, "The Staircase to Terrorism: A Psychological Exploration," *American Psychologist*, Vol. 60, No. 2, 2005, pp. 161–169; Fathali Moghaddam, *From the Terrorists' Point of View: What They Experience and Why They Come to Destroy*, Westport, Conn.: Praeger Security International, 2006; Marc Sageman, "A Strategy for Fighting International Islamist Terrorists," *Annals of the American Academy of Political and Social Science*, Vol. 618, No. 1, 2008, pp. 223–231; Silber and Bhatt, 2007, pp. 6–7; Quitan Wiktorowicz, "Joining the Cause: Al-Muhajiroun and Radical Islam," paper presented at the Roots of Islamic Radicalism Conference, Yale University, 2004. See also King and Taylor, 2011, pp. 604–608.

[7]   King and Taylor, 2011, pp. 604–612.

In the context of the current study, it is important to note that many persons analyzed did not necessarily complete the general progression sketched above. Some, for instance, may have played roles as financiers or facilitators but had no intention of ever personally conducting an act of terrorism. Others' progression down this path may have been artificially accelerated by the influence of cooperating government informants and/or undercover law enforcement agents. Still others may have abandoned the path and been arrested retroactively for past plots, or been genuinely destined to complete the path but were arrested before the journey to terrorism was complete. Silber and Bhatt have noted, however, that even though not everyone who begins this process will conduct a terrorist attack, it does not mean they are no longer a threat: "Individuals who have been radicalized but are not jihadists may serve as mentors and agents of influence to those who might become the terrorists of tomorrow."[8]

The Cyclical Pattern of Arrests Since 9/11

In 2015, as ISIL reached the peak of its terroristic brutality, the number of U.S. persons arrested on crimes related to terrorism spiked to its highest level ever in the post-9/11 era (71 in total). Notably, though, the annual statistics on unsealed indictments seems to reveal a roughly cyclical pattern of arrests with spikes occurring in 2002–2003, 2009–2010, and 2015–2016. Of the 420 total arrests made in the 16-year period examined in this study, fully 60 percent occurred in these six years alone (see Figure 2.1).

The data in Figure 2.1 is incomplete for years 2001 and 2017, as our sample ran from September 12, 2001 to September 2017. Further, as noted above, data on the identities of U.S. FFs abroad, particularly in Iraq and Syria, is notoriously difficult to collect for a number of reasons. Unless a U.S. citizen holds a prominent leadership role in an FTO (as was the case for the now-deceased Anwar al-Awlaki and Adam Gadahn), is publicly recognized as a martyr posthumously by the FTO, or is identified in court filings in association with other indicted terrorists, U.S. intelligence and law enforcement agencies—as well as the FTO and the individual himself—typically have strong motives to avoid disclosure of rank-and-file terrorists abroad. Thus, in Figure 2.1, the absolute number of U.S. FFs known to have traveled abroad in a given year who remain at large should be viewed as a significant underestimate. Still, some trends can be gleaned from the limited data that is available at an unclassified level.

While it is impossible to attribute any causal links to this statistical observation, several drivers may come into play. It should be noted that the increased activities during these periods could reflect an increase in law enforcement activity resulting in more arrests, an increase in real terrorist activity resulting in more arrests, or both. In the climate of fear following 9/11, for instance, the years 2002–2003 saw a massive increase in federal resources devoted to uncovering potential plots, as well as profile-driven investigations of the Muslim American community, on a historically unprec-

---

[8] Silber and Bhatt, 2007, p. 10.

Figure 2.1
Annual Number of U.S. Persons Arrested, Killed in Action, or Who Fled Abroad, 2001–2017

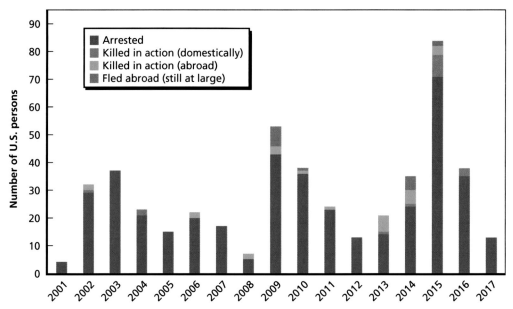

NOTES: The data in Figure 2.1 is incomplete for years 2001 and 2017, as our sample ran from September 12, 2001 to September 2017. Further, as noted above, data on the identities of U.S. foreign fighters abroad, particularly in Syria and Iraq, is notoriously difficult to collect for a number of reasons. Unless a U.S. citizen holds a prominent leadership role in an FTO (such as the cases of the now-deceased Adam Gadahn and Anwar al-Awlaki), is publicly recognized as a martyr posthumously by the FTO, or is identified in court filings in association with other indicted terrorists, U.S. intelligence and law enforcement agencies—as well as the FTO and individual himself—typically have strong motives to avoid disclosure of rank-and-file terrorists abroad. Thus, in Figure 2.1, the absolute number of U.S. foreign fighters known to have traveled abroad in a given year who remain at large should be viewed as a significant underestimate; still, some trends can be gleaned from the limited data that are available at an unclassified level.

edented scale. Almost two-thirds of those arrested in these years were indicted on charges of financing or facilitating terror groups through other forms of material support; relatively few individuals were indicted on charges pertaining to actual planned or materialized plots during this first post-9/11 spike in domestic arrests. This trend will be discussed in more detail later in this report.

By contrast, by 2009 the threat of so-called lone wolf attacks began to be recognized as arguably the principal threat to the U.S. homeland.[9] Indeed, according to our analysis, the number of arrests of HVEs jumped from zero in 2008 to 17 in 2009. In

---

[9]   On al Qaeda's adaptation during this period in response to a decade of unrelenting global counterterrorism operations—namely, its shifting focus from conducting large-scale attacks in the West to seeking "American homegrown recruits to implement a campaign of individual jihad and do-it-yourself terrorism," see Jenkins, 2011.

part, this new wave of homegrown terrorism reflects the incursion of al Qaeda into a variety of affiliated movements, and its efforts to inspire small-scale, independent attacks in the name of jihad. It can also be correlated with evolutions in the use of the internet by FTOs, as social media platforms such as Facebook, Instagram, Twitter, and YouTube replaced private password-protected websites as the most utilized tools for FTO propaganda and information operations.[10] After 9/11 there was an exponential increase in the volume of public FTO websites and social media accounts as encryption tools proliferated, private-sector tech companies battled government pressure to violate user privacy agreements, and FTOs commensurately came to view the rewards of utilizing mass electronic platforms as outweighing the risks.[11] According to cyberterrorism expert Gabriel Weimann, for instance, the number of terrorist-operated websites exploded from less than 100 in 1998 (including about half of the 30 U.S.-designated FTOs) to approximately 4,300 in by 2005; this trend paralleled the spike in worldwide use of the internet, from some 60 million users in the mid-1990s to over one billion in the early years of the twenty-first century.[12] As many official and unofficial terrorist-operated websites fell under increasing surveillance and attack from intelligence and law enforcement agencies, "their operators [were forced] to seek new online alternatives . . . [and] the turn to social media followed."[13] These new media platforms were particularly popular among younger demographics. They enabled two-way communication

---

[10] On evolution of the use of the internet by terrorist and insurgent organizations, see, for instance, Gabriel Weimann, *New Terrorism and New Media*, Research Series Vol. 2, Washington, D.C.: Woodrow Wilson International Center for Scholars, 2014; Seth G. Jones, *Waging Insurgent Warfare: Lessons from the Vietcong to the Islamic State*, New York: Oxford University Press, 2017, pp. 122–130; Steven Metz, "The Internet, New Media, and the Evolution of Insurgency," *Parameters*, Vol. 42, No. 3, Autumn 2012, pp. 80–90; Audrey Kurth Cronin, "Cyber-Mobilization: The New *Levée en Masse*," *Parameters*, Vol. 36, No. 2, Summer 2006, pp. 77–87; Eben Kaplan, "Terrorists and the Internet," Council on Foreign Relations, January 8, 2009; and Bruce Hoffman, "The Use of the Internet by Islamic Extremists," testimony before the House Permanent Select Committee on Intelligence, May 4, 2006.

[11] Gabriel Weimann summarizes these rewards as including "easy access; little or no regulation, censorship, or other forms of government control; potentially huge audiences spread throughout the world [including current and potential supporters, international public opinion, and enemy publics]; anonymity of communication; a fast flow of information; inexpensive development and maintenance of a web presence; a multimedia environment (the ability to combine text, graphics, audio, and video and to allow users to download films, songs, books, posters, and so forth); and the ability to shape coverage in the traditional mass media, which increasingly use the Internet as a source for stories." He further observes that the internet serves at least eight functions for modern terrorist organizations: propagandizing, recruiting, training, fund-raising, networking, planning and coordinating terrorist attacks, data mining and intelligence gathering (e.g., on potential attack targets, government counterterrorism tactics and strategies, etc.), and conducting psychological warfare. Gabriel Weimann, *www.terror.net: How Modern Terrorism Uses the Internet*, Special Report 116, Washington, D.C.: U.S. Institute of Peace, March 2004, pp. 1–3.

[12] Gabriel Weimann, *Terror on the Internet: The New Arena, the New Challenges*, Washington, D.C.: USIP Press Books, March 2006; Weimann, 2004, pp. 3–5, 15.

[13] Weimann, 2014, p. 2.

as opposed to "one-to-many" communication; were "user-friendly, reliable, and free"; and permitted FTOs to "knock on [potential recruits'] doors" instead of waiting passively for target audiences to come to them.[14] Even by 2006, when today's social media giants like Facebook and Twitter were still in their infancy, an estimated "90 percent of terrorist activity on the Internet [was taking] place using social networking tools, be it independent bulletin boards, Paltalk, or Yahoo! eGroups."[15] In the second decade of the twenty-first century, these trends have accelerated as the use of mobile technologies and smartphones has proliferated and has increasingly penetrated new markets, particularly in Africa, the Middle East, and Southeast Asia. More recently, for instance, the Brookings Institution found that around the peak of ISIL's territorial control in Iraq and Syria in the autumn of 2014, at least 45,000 Twitter accounts were in use by ISIL members and supporters.[16]

Finally, as ISIL emerged as a new influence both actively and passively dominating the process of radicalization experienced by individuals in the United States, patterns in domestic arrests correspondingly reflected this changing nature of the threat environment; as is shown in Figure 2.1, a third post-9/11 spike occurred in 2015–2016. Of 106 individuals indicted on terrorism-related charges in that period, seven out of ten were either HVEs (38 total) or aspiring foreign fighters (AFFs; 36 total). In 2015–2016 an additional ten HVEs were killed by police in high-profile domestic attacks. Perhaps unsurprisingly, however, as coalition forces began to consolidate military gains against ISIL in Iraq and Syria in late 2016 and early 2017—and as ISIL subsequently continued to witness sharp declines in territorial control, financial resources, popular support, and propaganda output—U.S. domestic arrests of HVEs and AFFs decreased commensurately; through the period January–September 2017, DOJ announced the indictment of only four ISIL-inspired AFFs and five ISIL-inspired HVEs.[17]

The Prevalence of U.S.-Born Jihadist Terrorists

Overwhelmingly, most persons indicted on terrorism charges or who have become jihadist terrorists since 9/11 are U.S. citizens. Of the 476 individuals contained in this

---

[14] Weimann, 2014, pp. 2–3.

[15] Counterterrorism expert Evan Kohlmann, quoted in Yuki Noguchi, "Tracking Terrorists Online," *Washington Post*, April 19, 2006.

[16] J. M. Berger, "The Evolution of Terrorist Propaganda: The Paris Attack and Social Media," testimony before the House of Representatives Committee on Foreign Affairs, January 27, 2015.

[17] On the weakening of ISIL and its impact on radicalization and recruitment of U.S. persons, see, for instance, Charlie Winter, *ICSR Insight: The ISIS Propaganda Decline*, London: International Centre for the Study of Radicalisation and Political Violence, March 23, 2017a; Stefan Heibner, Peter Neumann, John Holland-McCowan, and Rajan Basra, *Caliphate in Decline: An Estimate of Islamic State's Financial Fortunes*, London: International Centre for the Study of Radicalisation and Political Violence, 2017; Colin P. Clarke, "The Terrorist Diaspora: After the Fall of the Caliphate," testimony before the House Homeland Security Committee Task Force on Denying Terrorists Entry into the United States, July 13, 2017; and Jones et al., 2017.

Figure 2.2
Total Percentage and Annual Number of U.S. Jihadist Terrorists by Citizenship Status, 2001–2017

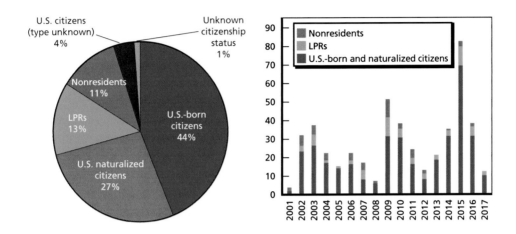

data set, 209 (44 percent) were born in the United States. An additional 129 were born abroad and became naturalized U.S. citizens, and 18 others were U.S. citizens of unknown status.[18] Collectively, therefore, about three-quarters of individuals consti-tuting the domestic terrorist threat have historically lived in the United States either since birth or long enough to complete the arduous naturalization process (see Figure 2.2).[19] Of the remaining 138 persons studied, 62 (13 percent) were LPRs at the time of their arrest or terrorism-related crime; 52 (11 percent) were nonresidents, including for-eign citizens on temporary visas, asylum seekers, and illegal aliens; 6 (1 percent) were of unknown citizenship status.

Notably, of the total nonresident population examined in this study, only 19 per-sons were discovered to be in the country illegally.[20] Similarly, of the 26 individuals responsible for the 23 domestic attacks in the United States since 9/11, only two were nonresidents, both of whom entered the country legally; by contrast, 13 were U.S. born, seven were naturalized U.S. citizens, and four were LPRs.

---

[18] To put this figure in perspective, on average an estimated 688,000 people are naturalized in the United States every year. In the 16 years since 9/11, therefore, about 11 million new citizens have been naturalized; U.S. Citi-zenship and Immigration Services, 2017.

[19] Between 2005 and 2014, the median number of years persons spent in LPR status before completing the naturalization process ranged from six to nine years. See Nadwa Mossaad and James Lee, "U.S. Naturalizations: 2014," Annual Flow Report, Washington, D.C.: U.S. Department of Homeland Security, April 2016.

[20] The majority of these 19 individuals had illegally overstayed their visas; only four were confirmed to have entered the country illegally, three of whom did so as children.

The Rise of American HVEs, AFFs, and FFs

For each individual contained in the data set, we coded that person's primary role in terrorist activity along a spectrum of six designations: (1) FF, defined as a U.S. citizen or resident who successfully traveled abroad to join an FTO; (2) AFF, defined as a U.S. citizen or resident who attempted to travel abroad to join an FTO, but who was arrested prior to arriving at the foreign battlefield or training camp, or who otherwise failed to reach his or her destination; (3) HVE, defined as an individual inside the United States who plotted or conspired to conduct a terrorist attack domestically but who was not explicitly directed to do so by an FTO; (4) direct terrorist operative (DTO), defined as an individual within the United States—or a foreign agent operationally inbound to the United States—who sought and/or attempted to conduct a terrorist attack on U.S. soil at the explicit direction of FTO leadership; (5) financier, defined as a U.S. person who raised and donated money on behalf of an FTO; and (6) facilitator, defined as a U.S. person who provided primarily nonmonetary support to an FTO—such as equipment or propaganda/recruiting services—or who provided material support to HVEs, FFs, and/or AFFs, including logistical travel assistance to battlefields abroad. It should be noted that in approximately 10 percent of cases an individual could arguably have fit into multiple categories.[21] As a general rule, when confronted with such coding dilemmas, we have aimed for a standard of consistency and transparency by designating the person with the role appropriate to the most egregious of his or her offenses. We recognize, however, that these coding decisions might necessarily introduce an additional element of subjectivity and/or bias in the statistical findings of this report.[22]

Overall, since September 2001 the roles of U.S. persons who committed acts of terrorism or who have been indicted on terrorism-related charges has been fairly evenly

---

[21] As one recent illustration, for instance, in March 2017 U.S.-born citizen Zakaryia Abdin was arrested at Charleston International Airport attempting to board a plane to fly overseas to join ISIL. This was not, however, Abdin's first run-in with the law on terrorism-related charges; he was first arrested in 2015 at the age of 16 for plotting to kill American soldiers in the United States. Though then sentenced to five years in juvenile detention, Abdin was paroled in May 2016. In this case, we coded Abdin's primary role as an AFF rather than an HVE based on the logic that he never operationalized the earlier plot and would surely face stricter sentencing guidelines if convicted of the later charges. As an alternative example, the distinction between financier and facilitator is often very thin. Take, for instance, the case of four Ohio men—Ibrahim Zubair Mohammad, Yahya Farooq Mohammad, Asif Ahmed Salim, and Sultane Room Salim—who were indicted on charges of conspiracy to provide financial and other types of support, including equipment and recruiting, to Anwar al-Awlaki and AQAP. Because the financial support was substantial—in excess of $22,000—we designated these individuals as financiers primarily rather than facilitators.

[22] While an in-depth, case study–level examination of these mixed-role individuals is beyond the scope of the present study, we recognize that this phenomenon is worth future examination to better understand trends in the personal evolution of U.S. persons' draw to foreign terrorism—that is, how U.S. citizens might begin engaging with an FTO as, say, a financier or facilitator and then transition to an AFF, or how one might begin with a domestic orientation as an HVE and then travel overseas to become an FF.

Figure 2.3
Total Percentage and Annual Number of U.S. Jihadist Terrorists by Role, 2001–2017

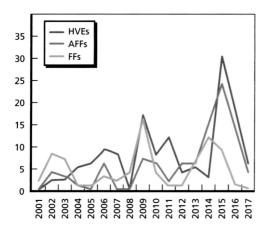

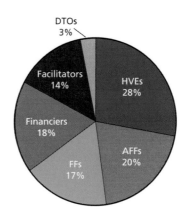

distributed across these categories: 136 persons (28 percent) can best be characterized as HVEs, 95 persons (20 percent) as AFFs, 79 persons (17 percent) as FFs, 85 persons (18 percent) as financiers, and 68 persons (14 percent) as facilitators (see Figure 2.3).[23] Remarkably, our research identified only 13 persons who had acted as direct operatives of FTOs in the last 16 years, perhaps defying post-9/11 conventional wisdom regarding the prevalence of foreign terrorist agents operating in the U.S. homeland under the direct orders and with the material support of FTO leadership. While this finding should not be interpreted as diminishing the persistent threat posed to the U.S. homeland by FTOs such as AQAP,[24] which continues to aspire to execute catastrophic external operations in the West, it does reinforce the narrative that the U.S. intelligence, security, and immigration apparatuses have proven resilient since 9/11. Relatedly, it

---

[23] For reasons noted above, obtaining accurate numbers on the identities of U.S. persons who have traveled abroad to become FFs is virtually impossible at the unclassified level. Based on overall estimates provided in public testimony by top U.S. government officials, we judge this figure to be significantly lower than the reality, particularly since the rise of ISIL in 2013.

[24] According to many analysts, AQAP remains the most imminent great threat to the security of the U.S. homeland. As terrorist expert Daniel Byman explains, "In the past, when an affiliate joined Al Qaeda, it usually took on more regional activities and went after more international targets in its region, but did not focus on attacks in the West. Only one affiliate—AQAP—prioritized striking the U.S. homeland and Europe." Byman further explains the differing threat profiles of al Qaeda and its affiliates versus ISIL: While the former continues to pursue a "'far enemy' strategy," the latter is focused on a "'near enemy' strategy, albeit on a regional level." He thus argues that "Al Qaeda and its affiliates remain a threat to the U.S. homeland, while the Islamic State's danger is more to the stability of the Middle East and U.S. interests overseas." See Daniel Byman, "Comparing Al Qaeda and ISIS: Different Goals, Different Targets," testimony before the Subcommittee on Counterterrorism and Intelligence of the House Committee on Homeland Security, April 29, 2015.

also underscores the insight that—in light of the many obstacles faced by foreign terrorist networks in delivering their own sleeper agents or direct operatives to American shores—FTOs like al Qaeda and ISIL have adapted by focusing their influence
inward, on vulnerable populations within the United States. Figure 2.3 illustrates this
trend quantitatively. As has been alluded to above, it shows the upward trend in domestic radicalization of HVEs since 9/11, as well as the increasing draw of U.S. persons to
travel abroad to become FFs. Note that given the aforementioned problems inherent
in collecting unclassified data on the identity of rank-and-file U.S. FFs (particularly
those in Iraq and Syria), the patterns presented in Figure 2.3 likely underrepresent the
upward trend since 2013 in this segment of the population; in reality, the spike in FFs
(the green trend line) probably mirrors or even exceeds the spikes documented in AFFs
and HVEs (the blue and red trend lines).

Other Demographic Profile Trends

Not surprisingly, the overall composition of the population examined was found to be
overwhelmingly male (93 percent) and relatively young (30 years old, on average).[25]
Notably, however, the average age of U.S. jihadist terrorists has seemingly been in
decline; whereas the mean age of persons in our data set averaged 35–37 years of age
in 2002–2005, this figure dropped to approximately 25–26 years of age in 2014–2015
(see Figure 2.4). This may likely be a reflection of the previously noted changing roles
of jihadist terrorists—that is, the relative increase in HVEs, AFFs, and FFs in recent

---

[25] This result is unsurprising given that demographic studies on U.S. domestic terrorist profiles have consistently
found this population to be mostly male and young. It is somewhat less well understood *why* the population
tends to be younger and overwhelmingly male, and a variety of theories have been postulated. For example, some
observers suggest that younger individuals are strategically targeted by terrorist recruiters, perhaps because of
their perceived ideological malleability. As Anthony Faiola and Souad Mehhennet write, "[ISIL recruiters] groom
children much the way pedophiles do—deploying flattery and attention while pretending to be friends"; Anthony
Faiola and Souad Mehhennet, "What's Happening to Our Children?" *Washington Post*, February 11, 2017. Some
experts suggest there may exist cognitive developmental and neurobiological explanations: adolescents tend to
engage in more high-risk activity because their prefrontal cortex has not yet developed fully; the reward pathways
in young adult brains light up differently than older brains; surges of testosterone may increase aggressive and
violent tendencies in young men rather than young women. Some social scientists posit that younger populations
are inherently more idealistic; seek status recognition and group identity; have fewer constraining familial and
professional obligations; and are more vulnerable to promises of glory, adventure, and purpose. Some observers
argue that social norms, roles, and expectations might be a strong causal factor in the observed gender discrepancies in terrorist profiles, particularly among traditionally conservative communities. Still others point to the challenges inherent in restrictions on law enforcement and intelligence agencies' ability to monitor minors because
of domestic laws protecting children. See, for instance, John M. Venhaus, *Why Youth Join al-Qaeda*, Special
Report 236, Washington, D.C.: U.S. Institute of Peace, May 2010; Meredith Melnick, "Why Are Terrorists So
Often Young Men?" *Huffington Post*, April 23, 2013; Maggie Penman and Shankar Vedantam, "The Psychology
of Radicalization: How Terrorist Groups Attract Young Followers," National Public Radio, December 15, 2015;
New America, "Terrorism in America After 9/11: Part II. Who Are the Terrorists?" undated; and Karen Jacques
and Paul Taylor, "Myths and Realities of Female-Perpetrated Terrorism," *Law and Human Behavior*, Vol. 37, No.
1, 2013, pp. 35–44.

years compared to the predominance of prosecutions of financiers and facilitators in the immediate post-9/11 years. On average, HVEs, AFFs, and FFs tend to be significantly younger (26 years old) than financiers and facilitators (37 years old).[26]

Ethnically and racially, individuals of Middle Eastern, North African, and/or South Central Asian descent comprise the largest demographic share (206 individuals), though African American/black and Caucasian/white demographics were also well represented: 137 and 74 persons, respectively.[27] Somewhat surprisingly, however, in percentage terms the number of individuals of Middle Eastern, North African, and/or South Central Asian descent has declined in recent years relative to other demographics; in 2014–2016, for instance, the combined African American and Caucasian population made up 79 percent, 57 percent, and 62 percent of cases by year. Perhaps relatedly, the years 2013–2015 were marked by a noticeable increase in the number of Muslim converts who were arrested on terrorism-related charges or committed acts of terrorism (see Figure 2.4). In total, 130 individuals in our data set were confirmed as having converted to Islam; of these converts, 48 arrests/attacks occurred in 2013–2015.[28]

Geographically per capita, the United States is essentially well represented in the population of individuals examined in this study: the 476 persons examined came from hometowns in 37 states. Eleven states accounted for three-fourths of the population: New York (76 persons), California (42 persons), Minnesota (38 persons), Virginia (38 persons), Florida (29 persons), Texas (25 persons), Illinois (24 persons), Ohio (21 persons), Michigan (20 persons), North Carolina (17 persons), and New Jersey (16 persons). These eleven states constituted 10 of the top 12 most populous states in America in 2016, with the only outlier being Minnesota (see Box 2.1), which ranked twenty-

---

[26] Broken down further, the mean age for 135 HVEs in our data set was 27 years (median age, 25 years); for 95 AFFs it was 25 years (median age, 22 years); for 77 FFs it was 27 years (median age, 27 years); for 82 financiers it was 40 years (median age, 41 years); and for 66 facilitators it was 34 years (median age, 31 years). While an in-depth probe of the causal mechanisms underlying these average age discrepancies by role is beyond the scope of the present study, at least a couple of explanations seem plausible. First, older persons may tend to be more financially stable than younger ones, and thus possess greater means to contribute significant financial and material resources as sympathizers, particularly among the diaspora community. On average, they may also be more risk averse due to constraints imposed by familial responsibilities, professional commitments, community ties, and even physical health limitations. By contrast, as noted in greater detail in the preceding note, younger recruits may be comparatively drawn to operational roles (i.e., risk-taking behavior) due to a bevy of social, psychological, ideological, and even biological factors such as adventure-seeking and status-seeking tendencies, naive idealism, premature cognitive development, and so forth. These, of course, are speculative explanations based only on anecdotal evidence and should not be interpreted as generalizable to the population as a whole.

[27] Out of 476 individuals, ethnic/racial codings could not be determined for 24 persons.

[28] It should be noted that convert data were unavailable for 37 of 476 individuals.

second in population in 2016.[29] Of the 13 states not represented, all numbered in the 20 least populous states in America in 2016.[30]

As regards education, our data suggest that approximately three-fourths of radicalized U.S. persons obtain less than a college degree. While it should be cautioned that we could only collect educational data on about half of the individuals in the data set, we found that 38 percent received a high school degree or lower level of education; 37 percent attended some college or received an associate's degree; 14 percent received a bachelor's degree; and 11 percent completed at least some graduate-level studies. Perhaps counterintuitively, these education attainment levels are remarkably similar to the U.S. population as a whole.[31]

Although the proportion of female jihadist terrorists among the population remains low, the number of women arrested on terrorism-related charges spiked notably in 2014–2015; 60 percent of all women contained in the data set were arrested in these two years alone.[32] The female jihadist terrorist profile differs from the male profile in several other respects. Of the 32 women represented, 27 (84 percent) were Caucasian/white (including Hispanic) or African American/black, compared to only 5 women of Middle Eastern, North African, or South Central Asian descent. Fully 82 percent were U.S. citizens (19 U.S. born, seven naturalized); one-third had converted to Islam; and only two women were HVEs (compared to 17 women as financiers or facilitators and 13 as AFFs or FFs).

---

[29] U.S. Census Bureau, "State Population Tables: 2010–2016," webpage, undated, b.

[30] Those states not represented include Delaware, Iowa, Maine, Montana, Nebraska, Nevada, New Hampshire, New Mexico, North Dakota, South Dakota, Utah, Vermont, and West Virginia.

[31] According to the U.S. Census Bureau, in 2011 approximately 43 percent of the U.S. population received a high school degree or lower level of education, 26 percent attended some college or received an associate's degree, 19 percent held a bachelor's degree, and 10 percent held a master's or higher degree; U.S. Census Bureau, *Educational Attainment: Five Key Data Releases from the U.S. Census Bureau*, Washington, D.C.: U.S. Census Bureau, undated, a. While some scholars argue that lack of education may have a causal impact on radicalization, many others refute this claim. On the complex link between education levels and political violence, see, for instance, Sarah Brockhoff, Tim Krieger, and Daniel Meierrieks, "Great Expectations and Hard Times: The (Non-Trivial) Impact of Education on Domestic Terrorism," *Journal of Conflict Resolution*, Vol. 59, No. 7, 2015, pp. 1186–1215; Alexander Lee, "Who Becomes a Terrorist? Poverty, Education, and the Origins of Political Violence," *World Politics*, Vol. 63, No. 2, April 2011, pp. 203–245; Alan Kreuger, "Education, Poverty, and Terrorism: Is There a Causal Connection?" *Journal of Economic Perspectives*, Vol. 17, No. 4, 2003, pp. 119–144; Faheem Akhter, "Education, Dialogue, and Deterrence: Tools for Counter Terrorism," *Sociology and Anthropology*, Vol. 4, No. 4, 2016, pp. 257–262; Clayton Thyne, "ABCs, 123s, and the Golden Rule: The Pacifying Effect of Education on Civil War, 1980–1999," *International Studies Quarterly*, Vol. 50, No. 4, 2006, pp. 733–754; Claude Berrebi, "Evidence About the Link Between Education, Poverty, and Terrorism Among Palestinians," *Peace Economics, Peace Science, and Public Policy*, Vol. 13, No. 1, January 2007, pp. 1–36; and Jessica Stern, "Pakistan's Jihad Culture," *Foreign Affairs*, Vol. 79, No. 6, November–December 2000, pp. 115–126.

[32] See Audrey Alexander, "A Year After San Bernardino, the Number of Women Jihadis Is Growing," Lawfare, December 18, 2016.

Figure 2.4
Demographic Trends in U.S. Jihadist Terrorists by Age, Race/Ethnicity, and Religious Conversion, 2001–2017

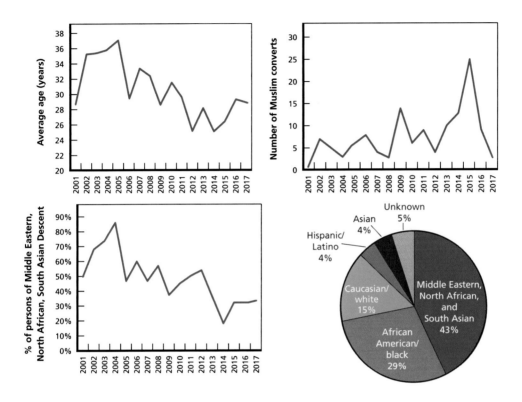

Comparative Analysis of the Draw to al Qaeda and ISIL

In the sections that follow, we look more specifically at trends in the data broken down between al Qaeda and ISIL—as well as other groups—in order to identify possible differences in the segments of the population touched by each organization. Our goal is to inform a more nuanced understanding of changing patterns in the draw of U.S. persons to different FTOs in the post-9/11 era.

The Crowding Out of al Qaeda and Its Affiliates

In the decade and a half since the declaration of America's global war on terror, al Qaeda and its related offshoot movements have developed in roughly three phases. First, as U.S. forces aggressively hunted al Qaeda in the early post-9/11 years, the organization and its foreign influence remained dominated by its core leadership, which consolidated its base of operations in Pakistan. Second, from roughly 2004 to 2012, the organization spread its reach beyond Afghanistan and Pakistan, adding five official affiliate groups—AQI in 2004, AQAP and al Qaeda in the Islamic Maghreb in

Box 2.1. A Portrait of the Somali Diaspora in U.S. Jihadist Terrorist Trends

In January 1991 the government of Somali dictator Mohamed Siad Barre collapsed in a military coup after two decades in power, unleashing a complex civil war between a succession of rival clans, warlords, insurgent groups, and terrorist organizations that would persist nearly uninterrupted to the present day. As U.S. forces landed the following year in their first major post–Cold War military intervention, an estimated one-third to two-thirds of the population of 7.5 million were at risk of dying from a famine, and some 2 million to 3.5 million had become refugees or internally displaced persons. Over the subsequent decades, vulnerable populations from Somalia would become one of the largest immigrant communities from sub-Saharan Africa in the United States.[1]

Since 9/11, at least 55 individuals from the U.S. Somali diaspora community—including 36 from the Minneapolis–St. Paul, Minnesota, area—have been arrested on terrorism-related charges, have successfully traveled abroad to join an FTO, or have committed a domestic terrorist attack. These periods of radicalization occurred essentially in two clear waves with different profile characteristics: 2008–2011 (involving at least 26 persons) and 2014–2016 (also involving at least 26 persons). We highlight these statistics in extra detail because the Somali diaspora community has been the subject of intense academic, media, and political scrutiny with regard to debates over both national immigration policy and broader strategies to mitigate the draw of disaffected American youths to FTOs.

In the first wave, which directly corresponded with the heyday of al Qaeda's affiliate in Somalia, all but one individual was associated with or inspired by al Shabaab.[2] Notably, none was a U.S.-born citizen; the average age was 30 years (median age, 26 years); and, with one exception, all were either FFs (13 persons) or financiers/facilitators supporting al Shabaab materially (12 persons). Only one individual among this first-generation Somali immigrant community plotted to

---

[1]   Since the cycles of war and famine began in the early 1990s, approximately 1–1.5 million Somalis have emigrated abroad, including about 150,000 to the United States, of which more than 40,000 live in Minnesota. Notably, according to a 2013 study by the U.S. Census Bureau, 57.3 percent of Somali Americans are 24 years old or younger, with a median age of 21.2 years. See Richardson, 2011, p. 12; Southers and Heinz, 2015, pp. 1, 6; and U.S. Census Bureau, 2013 American Community Survey of Somalis 3-Yr Estimate, Washington, D.C.: U.S. Census Bureau, 2013.

[2]   For a detailed analysis of the rise and subsequent evolutionary phases of al Shabaab, see Seth G. Jones, Andrew Liepman, and Nathan Chandler, *Counterterrorism and Counterinsurgency in Somalia: Assessing the Campaign Against Al Shaba'ab*, Santa Monica, Calif.: RAND Corporation, RR-1539, 2016.

commit an attack domestically in the United States. Instead, their draw to an FTO was focused externally, rooted in an enduring connection to their country of birth.[3]

In the second wave, 60 percent were U.S.-born citizens. The average age was significantly younger: 22 years old (median age, 20 years). Only 3 persons out of 26 ever manifested clear al Shabaab sympathies and connections (two of whom were financiers). Rather, all but one of the other 23 were all connected with ISIL, and virtually all either became FFs (10 persons) or AFFs (12 persons).[4] Like the previous wave, however, relatively few conspired to commit an attack on U.S. soil (just three persons). As discussed in further detail below, these statistical insights from the microcosm of the Somali diaspora community reflect broader trends in the draw of U.S. persons to al Qaeda compared with ISIL, and may hold significant implications for U.S. policymakers.

---

[3] The only individual who attempted to commit a domestic terrorist attack (and is thus designated an HVE) during this first wave was Mohamed Osman Mohamud, the so-called Portland Christmas tree bomber. In several ways, Mohamud's profile differs from others in the Somali diaspora community during this period. Unlike many of the others, Mohamud came to the United States under refugee status as a toddler. As a teenager, he began to visit extremist websites and developed an electronic relationship with Samir Khan, who would later flee the United States to become the editor of *Inspire*, AQAP's English-language magazine. Mohamud was not, therefore, drawn by the call to return to Somalia to join al Shabaab, unlike other members of the Somali American community during this time. Instead Mohamud came under FBI scrutiny through the National Security Agency's electronic surveillance program, which was later disclosed by Edward Snowden and became the subject of an intricate federal government sting operation. A 19-year-old student at Oregon State University at the time of his arrest by undercover agents in December 2010, Mohamud's legal case has become one of the most high-profile cases in the post-9/11 era to invoke the "entrapment defense." See, for instance, Nicolas Medina Mora and Mike Hayes, "The Big (Imaginary) Black Friday Bombing," BuzzFeed News, November 15, 2014.

[4] The one exception became a foreign fighter with Jabhat al-Nusra in Syria.

2006, and al Shabaab and Jabhat al-Nusra in 2012—and increasingly reorienting its information operations and recruiting efforts toward audiences in the West. Finally, 2013 saw the evolution of AQI to ISIL; deepening divisions between the leadership of the ISIL and al Qaeda core in Pakistan; and growing rivalries between ISIL and Jabhat al-Nusra, culminating in outright interfactional fighting between the formerly allied affiliates in Iraq and Syria.

As is shown in Figure 2.5, the trends in the number of U.S. persons drawn to ISIL rather than al Qaeda and its offshoots have paralleled these developments. Indeed, since ISIL's official split from al Qaeda in 2014, it has virtually crowded out the recruitment successes of other FTOs; during this period, 150 U.S. persons have conspired to contribute materially to or act on behalf of ISIL, compared to just 9 for al Qaeda (excluding al Shabaab) and 11 for other organizations. Indeed, in its brief existence of less than five years, ISIL has succeeded in attracting more U.S. persons (32 percent of

Figure 2.5
Annual Number and Total Number of U.S. Jihadist Terrorists by Group, 2001–2017

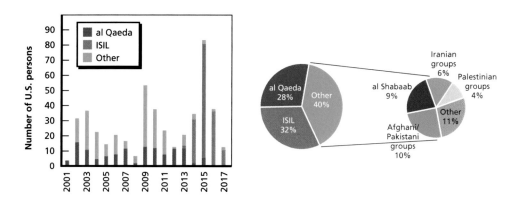

the total in our data set) than al Qaeda has since 9/11 (28 percent). By contrast, all other FTOs combined attracted the remaining 40 percent, with al Shabaab and groups in Afghanistan and Pakistan, such as the Taliban, leading this cohort.

Differing Jihadist Terrorist Profiles: Al Qaeda Versus ISIL

According to our data, since the rise of ISIL the demographic profile of the average U.S. person drawn to FTOs has changed in several significant ways. First, in both absolute and percentage terms, ISIL has overwhelmingly attracted more U.S.-born citizens than al Qaeda or any of its offshoot groups. Of the 152 individuals associated with ISIL in our data set, 106 (70 percent) were born in the United States, compared to just 59 of al Qaeda's total 131 U.S. persons (45 percent). By contrast, al Qaeda has attracted four times as many nonresidents (including individuals on visas and in the country illegally) as ISIL (20 persons versus 4 persons) and nearly twice as many naturalized U.S. citizens (37 persons versus 22 persons). Similarly, the non–ISIL/al Qaeda population represented in this data set is disproportionately composed of naturalized citizens, LPRs, and nonresidents (see Figure 2.6).

Second, U.S. persons drawn to ISIL have tended to adopt roles as FFs, AFFs, or HVEs in greater numbers than those historically drawn to al Qaeda. Figure 2.6 highlights these differences, though for reasons previously noted—namely, the impossibility of collecting comprehensive data on the exodus of U.S. citizens to Syria since 2013—it likely understates the trend. Additionally, in contrast to al Qaeda, ISIL has never deployed a DTO to the U.S. homeland, or at least none that is publicly known. It is notable as well that other groups—primarily FTOs located in Iran, Lebanon, Palestine, and Somalia—have attracted about three times as many financiers and facilitators than has ISIL.

Third, the segment of the U.S. population that has supported, joined, attempted to join, or pledged allegiance to ISIL has tended to be younger, less educated, and

Figure 2.6
Demographic Profiles of U.S. Jihadist Terrorists by Group, 2001–2017

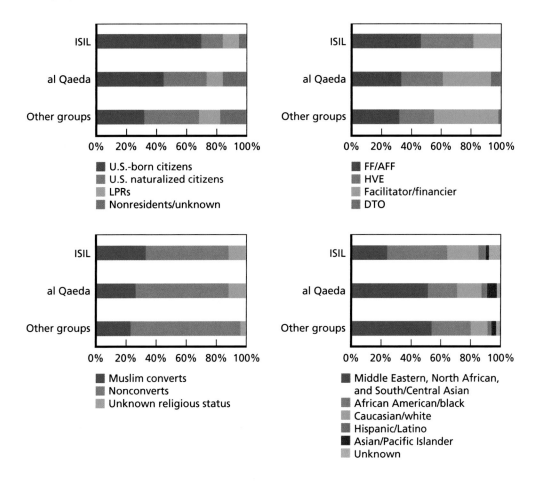

comprised of more Muslim converts and fewer individuals of Middle Eastern, North African, or South Central Asian descent than the share of the population historically drawn to al Qaeda or other FTOs. The typical ISIL recruit averaged 26.7 years of age at the time of his or her arrest, date of travel abroad, or death in a domestic attack; this compares to averages of 31.0 years and 32.1 years for al Qaeda and other groups, respectively. Only about 9 percent of U.S. persons associated with ISIL have achieved a bachelor's degree or engaged in graduate studies, compared to about 30 percent of U.S. persons connected to al Qaeda or other groups.[33] For those cases in which data are available, ISIL members are almost 10 percentage points more likely to be Muslim

---

[33] As previously noted, data on educational attainment could only be collected for about half of the persons in this study.

converts than are al Qaeda members.[34] Perhaps most notably, individuals radicalized by ISIL's influence have ethnically and racially not tended to be of Middle Eastern, North African, or South Central Asian descent; only 26 percent of persons fit this profile, compared to approximately 53 percent of al Qaeda recruits and supporters. Conversely, about 65 percent of U.S. persons drawn to ISIL since 2013 have been either African American/black or Caucasian/white.

---

[34] Data on conversion to Islam could not be collected for 37 out of the 476 persons (8 percent), of which 19 missing data points fell within the post-ISIL period (2013–2017) compared to five missing data points in the early years of al Qaeda (2001–2003) and 13 missing data points in al Qaeda's offshoot expansion period (2004–2012).

CHAPTER THREE

Conclusions

Our data analysis may hold useful implications for counterterrorism efforts, and particularly how to dedicate resources for law enforcement and intelligence operations and preventative measures such as countering violent extremism (CVE) programs. When orienting those efforts, it is very important to consider the changing demographic profile of terrorist recruits. This data analysis confirms some of the trends assumed in other literature, such as the profile of an ISIL recruit as younger and less educated.[1] However, it also reveals some trends that were previously unnoted, including those related to citizenship and race/ethnicity. The portrait that emerges from our analysis suggests that the historic stereotype of a Muslim, Arab, immigrant male as the most vulnerable to extremism is not representative of many terrorist recruits today. Instead, recruits are more likely to be Caucasian/white or African American/black; they are more likely to be U.S. born; and they are more likely to have converted to Islam as part of their radicalization process. Although they are still primarily male, they are increasingly likely to be female. And, perhaps most important, at present they are more likely to be drawn to or influenced by ISIL rather than al Qaeda or its affiliates during their process of radicalization and journey to terrorism.

The core question driving this study initially was to examine empirically whether ISIL has been more successful than al Qaeda in recruiting Americans, in part because it was reaching a different demographic profile. Our data analysis implies the answer to that question is yes. But this finding begs another question: Why? Although identifying the underlying reasons behind these trends was beyond the scope of our primary research question, we offer some possible explanations and contributing factors that could be investigated more systematically in future research.

First, some scholars and practitioners have pointed to deliberate decisionmaking differences in branding strategies as an explanation for different recruiting outcomes between ISIL and al Qaeda in recent years. Terrorism experts Colin P. Clarke and Steven Metz, for instance, suggest that al Qaeda has continued to frame itself as an

---

[1] Vidino and Hughes, 2015, similarly find ISIS recruits to be younger than those arrested on terrorism-related charges in the past.

exclusive terrorist "luxury brand," whereas ISIL has adopted a "big box retail outlet" branding strategy:

> ISIS's big box retail approach consists of several important variables: reach, consistency, its positioning as a loss leader, psychological appeal and freshness (or keeping things new and current). Al Qaida, as the luxury alternative, is more focused on exclusivity, pedigree, price-setting and seeking adherents who truly understand its message. . . . For [ISIL], it's a numbers game, both in focusing more on the quantity than the quality of attacks, but also in terms of reach and thus, recruitment. . . . [In contrast,] al Qaida is more selective and discerning about who it recruits and what targets it chooses to attack. The barriers to entry into al Qaida are higher, by design, to keep the uninvited at bay and maintain exclusivity of the brand.[2]

In other words, driven by different grand strategies—that is, al Qaeda's apparent preference to affect "ever-bigger and more dramatic attacks" compared with ISIL's pursuit of "killing as many helpless victims it can in relatively low-tech ways"[3]—the organizations' respective branding and recruiting methods have evolved in different ways.

Second, and relatedly, these strategic branding differences implicitly suggest that ISIL and al Qaeda purposefully target somewhat different ideological audiences. Clarke and Metz note that "al Qaida likely believes that recruits with actual knowledge of Quranic scripture are more serious about pursuing the organization's objectives and more in tune with its overall ideological goals and agenda."[4] At the same time, al Qaeda has positioned itself as the more moderate, preeminent brand of Salafi jihadism, frequently criticizing ISIL's brutal tactics for causing Muslim civilian casualties.[5] By contrast, ISIL's messaging has seemingly targeted a broader audience that may share a more generalized sense of social alienation and may be attracted to ISIL's comparatively extremist brand in and of itself. This hypothesis is consistent with past research that has suggested that "feelings of social alienation may contribute to the allure and power of radicalizing social groups."[6] It further suggests that the potential supply of recruits who find ISIL's extremist message may be larger, and more diverse, than that

---

[2] Colin P. Clarke and Steven Metz, "ISIS vs. Al Qaida: Battle of the Terrorist Brands," *National Interest*, August 16, 2016.

[3] Steven Metz, "Can the U.S. Counter Terrorism's Shift to Decentralized and Radicalized Violence?" *World Politics Review*, July 29, 2016.

[4] Clarke and Metz, 2016.

[5] Daveed Gartenstein-Ross and Nathaniel Barr, "Extreme Makeover, Jihadist Edition: Al-Qaeda's Rebranding Campaign," War on the Rocks, September 3, 2015.

[6] Todd C. Helmus, "Why and How Some People Become Terrorists," in Paul K. Davis and Kim Cragin, eds., *Social Science for Terrorism: Putting the Pieces Together,* Santa Monica, Calif.: RAND Corporation, MG-849-OSD, 2009.

of al Qaeda or other terrorist organizations that target narrower religious, racial, or nationalist ideologies and grievances. Taken together, these trends may explain why al Qaeda's past recruiting efforts overwhelmingly appealed to Middle Eastern Muslims and second-generation American Muslims who may have felt excluded and marginalized by the Western communities in which they reside, whereas ISIL's recruiting efforts today appear to appeal to more diverse demographic groups with varied sources of social alienation. If this is true, it has important implications for how future intervention and prevention efforts should be oriented.

Third, as ISIL rose to the height of its foreign recruiting strength in 2014–2016 it embraced communication tactics that differed, and in many ways were more sophisticated, from those of al Qaeda, giving the "group an edge over its rivals and [transforming] its war against the rest of the world."[7] Most saliently, the use of social media became comparatively more important to ISIL's recruiting operations.[8] Consistent with the aforementioned trends, while al Qaeda's core leadership has always maintained tight message control, ISIL's communication operations became largely decentralized at the caliphate's peak, with provincial media offices exercising relatively little message discipline—the implication of which being, "if this particular message doesn't appeal to you, don't worry, a different one will come along soon."[9] At the same time, ISIL furthered the earlier efforts of al Qaeda in the Arabian Peninsula to publish propaganda in English (and other languages) in its online magazine, *Dabiq*, as well as through its Amaq News Agency wire service. Consequently, the sheer volume of ISIL propaganda reaching foreign audiences far outpaced that of al Qaeda. More recently, as ISIL's territorial control and manpower have collapsed, its overall media output has declined "by about 90 percent compared with the summer of 2015, when it was at its height."[10] This in part may explain the notable decline in recruitment of U.S. persons to ISIL beginning in 2016, as observed in our data set.

Fourth, another potential reason for the rise, and possible peak, in ISIL's recruiting has been the role of momentum and the international media's complicity in drawing attention to the group's early successes. Simply stated, given rivalrous recruitment pressures, it is reasonable to expect U.S. persons to be drawn to the winner—to the organization that is growing, not waning, in strength and prestige. For instance, although al Qaeda called decades ago for the establishment of an Islamic state as a long-term goal, it has in its existence made little effort toward taking territory and

---

[7]   Charlie Winter, "What I Learned from Reading the Islamic State's Propaganda Instruction Manual," Lawfare, April 2, 2017.

[8]   Clarke and Metz, 2016.

[9]   Clarke and Metz, 2016.

[10]   Charlie Winter and Jade Parker, "Virtual Caliphate Rebooted: The Islamic State's Evolving Online Strategy," Lawfare, January 7, 2018.

governing. ISIL, in contrast, has found that its ability to rapidly take control of large areas of territory could become a self-reinforcing mechanism to gain recruits (and other forms of financial and political support and legitimacy), which in turn could lead to control over more territory and further gains in momentum. ISIL's declaration of a caliphate likely provided would-be recruits with a greater sense of belonging and/or purpose than al Qaeda's message of establishing a future Islamic state.[11] At the same time, Daveed Gartenstein-Ross and Nathaniel Barr have argued that al Qaeda leadership strategically encouraged and cultivated its image "as a dying organization" in order to understate its strength and "avoid drawing the attention of Western militaries and alleviating Gulf states' fears."[12] In other words, whether real or imagined, the proliferation of the perception that ISIL was gaining strength at al Qaeda's expense in zero-sum terms might have becoming a self-fulfilling prophesy, crowding out al Qaeda recruitment in 2014–2016. This explanation is consistent with the downward trend of new ISIL recruits in 2017–2018—particularly of AFFs—as ISIL's territorial control, financing, and momentum collapsed in Iraq and Syria.

Policy Implications

The historic stereotypical image of an FTO-linked terrorist, however, may persist in the minds of law enforcement and the public. As our analysis has shown, this was the dominant profile of individuals drawn to al Qaeda. It is therefore not unreasonable to think that individuals are consciously or unconsciously biased toward this profile, though such a bias could undermine future efforts to prevent terrorist acts. For example, CVE programs may be centered on engaging youth at mosques or in communities with a high population of recent immigrants. Campaigns to educate communities about how to identify the warning signs of radicalization or to promote the provision of tips and leads to law enforcement could be focused on the same populations. The national conversation on counterterrorism has often focused on enhancing screening of would-be refugees, asylum seekers, or visa holders or on tightening border controls to deny entry of would-be illegal aliens turned terrorists; however, these populations represented only a small fraction of our comprehensive data set. Effective counterterrorism programs would need to target the additional demographics identified by our research for people who are drawn to ISIL, such as native U.S. citizens with no preexisting connection to the Middle East or Islam.

The changing racial and national demographics of terrorist recruits also suggests that the draw of extremism does not appeal to something unique among the Muslim or

---

[11]   Daniel Byman and Jennifer R. Williams, "ISIS vs. Al Qaeda: Jihadism's Global Civil War," Brookings Institution, February 24, 2015.

[12]   Gartenstein-Ross and Barr, 2015.

Middle Eastern communities. Instead, the call to extremism—now much more accessible outside those communities thanks to FTO groups' use of social media—appeals to a small number of individuals from a variety of backgrounds.

The small number of FTO-related arrests and incidents in the United States is a limiting factor in how broadly conclusions should be drawn based on these data. However, our ability to do a comprehensive review of the nearly 500 cases related to Islamic FTOs since 9/11 does allow for other anecdotal, policy-relevant observations. One such observation reflects on the spectrum of threat presented by individuals connected to FTOs. Individuals who have successfully conducted a terrorist attack inside the United States leave a stark and fearsome image in the American psyche of the harm an inspired Islamist terrorist can do. The attacks in San Bernardino, California, and Orlando, Florida, in 2015 and 2016, respectively, are particularly vivid examples, although the mass shooting in Las Vegas in October 2017 is a reminder that terror often comes without any association to FTOs. Individuals such as Syed Rizwan Farook, Tashfeed Malik, Omar Mateen, and Tamerlan Tsarnaev, however, are not representative of many of the nearly 500 individuals arrested in connection with terrorism since 9/11. That is to say, our data set does not reflect the existence of 476 hardened jihadists inside the United States over the last 16 years. Beyond the fact that a portion of these individuals were facilitators and financiers who, though sympathetic to FTOs, likely had no intention of conducting a terrorist attack themselves, a great many attempts by those who sought to become terrorist operators have been unimpressive and amateurish. This assessment is consistent with a growing body of literature that has come to recognize that savvy, skilled, sophisticated domestic terrorists—persons like Mohamed Atta, one of the leaders of the 9/11 attacks—are the exception to the U.S. jihadist community.[13] As John Mueller and Mark Stewart conclude in their analysis of 50 post-9/11 U.S. jihadist case studies, the vast majority of individuals examined could fittingly be described as "incompetent, ineffective, unintelligent, idiotic, ignorant, inadequate, unorganized, misguided, muddled, amateurish, dopey, unrealistic, moronic, irrational, and foolish."[14] Moreover, as reflected in our "none ('jihad')" group coding, some individuals expressed only superficial sympathy for a terrorist organization, instead possibly seeking to aggrandize their violent deeds. Citing the example of two Western FFs who purchased *Islam for Dummies* from Amazon before departing for Syria in 2014 to join ISIL, terrorism expert Mia Bloom notes that many recent recruits drawn to global

---

[13] See, for instance, Daniel Byman and Christine Fair, "The Case for Calling Them Nitwits," *Atlantic*, July–August 2010; Mia Bloom, "Constructing Expertise: Terrorist Recruitment and 'Talent Spotting' in the PIRA, Al Qaeda, and ISIS," *Studies in Conflict & Terrorism*, Vol. 40, No. 7, 2017, pp. 603–623; and Bruce Schneier, "Portrait of the Modern Terrorist as an Idiot," *Wired News*, June 14, 2007.

[14] Mueller and Stewart, 2012, p. 88.

jihad "[do] not even know the most basic tenets of their own faith."[15] Also, while we did not systematically seek out information about potential mental illness, we noted suspected mental disorders in at least twenty cases; in these individuals this background risk factor may have influenced their path to radicalization more strongly than a profound political animosity toward the U.S. homeland or deep engagement with Islamist jihadist ideology, particularly in certain types of terrorists such as lone actors.[16] Furthermore, a great number of the individuals studied were lured to the call of jihad in Muslim lands abroad rather than domestically; whether adventure seekers or inspired by misguided senses of religious duty, they were not necessarily aggrieved with the U.S. homeland.[17] To date, no U.S. citizens who have traveled abroad to fight with ISIL have returned to the homeland to commit a domestic terror attack. In his influential study of Australian, North American, and Western European Islamist domestic and foreign fighters between 1990 and 2010, Thomas Hegghammer finds "that most Western jihadists prefer foreign fighting" and few Western FFs ever attempt to return home—though he notes that those who become returnees tend to be more lethal, direct operatives than the average HVEs.[18] He thus concludes,

---

[15] Bloom, 2017, p. 604. See also Mehdi Hasan, "What the Jihadists Who Bought 'Islam for Dummies' on Amazon Tell Us About Radicalisation," *New Statesman*, August 21, 2014. Quoting an analysis prepared by MI5's behavioral science unit, Hasan writes, "Far from being religious zealots, a large number of those involved in terrorism do not practice their faith regularly. Many lack religious literacy and could . . . be regarded as religious novices."

[16] The body of research on the relationship between the causal nature and prevalence of mental disorders and terrorist engagement has a long scholarly tradition, dating back to the late-1970s. However, in part because of the lack of scientific rigor and empirical evidence presented in the majority of these studies, there remains wide disagreement in the literature, with frequently cited works alternatively confirming or denying the existence of such relationships. Consequently, many false assumptions and incorrect conclusions have crept into both the popular and academic discourse on this subject. For a comprehensive review and critique of the history and evolution of these academic disagreements, see Gill and Corner, 2017, who conclude, "It is not true that terrorists share a common psychological profile. The evidence suggests however that some types of terrorists may be more likely to possess certain psychological traits more than the general population. The evidence also suggests that some types of terrorists [e.g., lone-actor terrorists] may also more likely possess certain psychological traits than other types of terrorists. The evidence also suggests that those terrorist subsamples with high rates of mental health disorders still fall below 50 percent. No mental health disorder appears to be a predictor of terrorist involvement. Terrorism remains a very low base-rate activity. Instead, for some terrorists the experience mental health disorders may be just one of many 'risk' factors that pushed and pulled that individual into terrorist engagement" (p. 239). See also Corner and Gill, 2017; Emily Corner, Paul Gill, and Oliver Mason, "Mental Health Disorders and the Terrorist: A Research Note Probing Selection Effects and Disorder Prevalence," *Studies in Conflict & Terrorism*, Vol. 39, No. 6, pp. 560–568; and Paul Gill, *Lone-Actor Terrorists: A Behavioural Analysis*, Abingdon, England: Routledge, 2015.

[17] For anecdotal evidence of this phenomenon, see, for instance, Marc Sageman, *Understanding Terrorist Networks*, Philadelphia: University of Pennsylvania Press, 2004.

[18] Thomas Hegghammer, "Should I Stay or Should I Go? Explaining Variation in Western Jihadists' Choice Between Domestic and Foreign Fighting," *American Political Science Review*, Vol. 107, No. 1, February 2013, p. 1, emphasis in the original.

Prosecuting all aspiring foreign fighters as prospective domestic terrorists has limited preventative benefits, because so few of them, statistically speaking, will go on to attack the homeland. By the same logic, the use of *agents provocateurs* to draw aspiring foreign fighters into fake domestic plots may have limited preventative value. By contrast, returning foreign fighters and their contacts should be monitored very carefully.[19]

This is not, of course, to dismiss the danger presented by terrorism in the United States but to ensure that this threat is put in appropriate perspective and that the complexity, variance, and nuance of terrorist behavior and motivation is understood and appreciated by policymakers. Failure to do so risks an improper alignment of limited law enforcement and intelligence resources, as well as misguided policy priorities and decisions.

The cyclical pattern of arrests observed in our findings is also notable; although, as just acknowledged, it would be premature to draw firm conclusions given the limited size of the population contained in our data set. ISIL could still adapt and resurge in creative ways. RAND terrorism experts Brian Michael Jenkins and Colin P. Clarke have hypothesized as to a few of such approaches, including an escalating offensive.[20] It would not be surprising if a new group emerged that attempted to recapitalize on the draw and momentum that ISIL demonstrated in 2015. Once again, if such a development were to occur, policymakers and intelligence and law enforcement officials would be wise to keep this development in proper perspective: the recurring spikes in our data—specifically, the subsequent case declines after jumps in 2009 and 2015—suggest that future surges can be similarly contained.

Furthermore, despite the evidence presented by this data set that U.S. persons have been drawn in far greater numbers to ISIL than to al Qaeda it recent years—the so-called crowding-out phenomenon—it would be a fallacy to conclude that ISIL recruits and operatives necessarily represent a greater danger to the U.S. homeland than do those of al Qaeda. A growing body of literature highlights the *quality* of human capital as an important factor in determining the productivity of terrorists.[21] To the extent that the historical data suggest that the typical profile of an al Qaeda recruit is older, better educated, and possibly more serious about the organization's objectives and ideological agenda than the average ISIL recruit, fewer, more capable al Qaeda

---

[19] Hegghammer, 2013, p. 13.

[20] Brian Michael Jenkins and Colin P. Clarke, "In the Event of the Islamic State's Untimely Demise . . . ," *Foreign Policy*, May 11, 2016.

[21] See, for instance, Ethan Bueno de Mesquita, "The Quality of Terror," *American Journal of Political Science*, Vol. 49, No. 3, 2005, pp. 515–530; Efraim Benmelech and Claude Berrebi, "Human Capital and the Productivity of Suicide Bombers," *Journal of Economic Perspectives*, Vol. 21, No. 3, 2007, pp. 223–238; and Efraim Benmelech, Claude Berrebi, and Esteban Klor, "Economic Conditions and the Quality of Suicide Terrorism," *Journal of Politics*, Vol. 74, No. 1, 2012, pp. 113–128.

conscripts might be more dangerous to the United States than more numerous, less capable ISIL ones. As Steven Metz argues, "The world must not become so focused on ISIL and its low-tech, limited-scale terrorism that it forgets that, in some dark corner of the world, al-Qaida is still plotting big, dramatic attacks."[22] Furthermore, the very real possibility exists that al Qaeda and ISIL could merge in the not-too-distant future, thus suggesting that CVE resources and attention should remain keenly focused on the former despite the proliferation of the latter.[23] In short, these considerations underscore the need for the law enforcement, intelligence, and military communities to exercise at least as much vigilance against the persistent threat posed by al Qaeda as by the rising threat posed by ISIL.

Areas for Future Research

A more thorough inquiry into this topic would benefit from the cooperation of law enforcement, and particularly the FBI. Although the FBI currently provides significant details about FTO-related arrests on the website of its National Security Branch, these press releases only go back to 2009. We have also identified some cases in the years after 9/11 for which there was very little or no information related in the public sphere. The FBI may be aware of additional cases that should be included among the data set, particularly in the earlier years. For the cases we have captured, the FBI may have additional information that could fill in gaps in our data set such as conversion to Islam, educational background, and past criminal history. A research project done in collaboration with law enforcement could also gauge whether some of the increases or decreases in arrests could reflect a change in the posture or priorities of law enforcement.

Our research also uses the date of arrests (or death, in applicable cases) to organize our data. However, a more precise query into how FTOs inspire terrorist actions would also consider the date when an individual began radicalizing, or at least when a law enforcement investigation was opened; ideally, it would probe the sequencing of the radicalization process of individuals in fine biographical detail. Some of this information can be ascertained from legal documents, such as the complaint or indictment. A research effort along these lines would be more intensive as these documents— although often public—can be difficult to find, are scanned and cannot be easily electronically searched, and/or contain varying levels of detail. However, incorporating these dates and data points would better reflect events that inspired an individual to conduct a terrorist act.

---

[22] Metz, 2016.

[23] Brian Michael Jenkins, "Could ISIS and Al Qaeda, Two Giants of Jihad, Unite?" Fox News, March 14, 2016.

Research efforts on this topic should also consider whether to include the entire population of domestic terrorists inside the United States. This could include individuals connected to white supremacists, sovereign citizens, militant environmentalists, revolutionary organizations, and the like. Doing so would require careful attention to definitions and coding criteria. Even the FBI acknowledges that there is "no single, universally accepted, definition of terrorism."[24] Whether to label the actions of individuals who conduct an act of mass murder as terrorism when there is no connection to an FTO or overt political motive is sometimes an issue of controversy. This issue recently came to the fore with Stephen Paddock's attack in Las Vegas in October 2017, as law enforcement has yet to determine the shooter's motivation.[25] Some of those arguing that the event should not be considered a terrorist event, such as Masha Gessen in the *New Yorker*, maintain that a terrorist event necessitates a political objective, which has not yet been demonstrated in the case of Paddock.[26] Gessen rightly points out that a political motivation is generally a component of any definition of terrorism, including that used by the FBI and in public law. However, a careful look at many of the cases in this case set would likely show a tenuous connection of the perpetrator to the FTO and its political goals. Almost all of the cases of terrorism since 9/11 are those of individuals inspired by these groups rather than individuals specifically directed by these groups to conduct a terrorist act. Most who claim to act on behalf of al Qaeda or ISIL never actually establish contact with those groups. Rather, group identity is often seemingly more fluid, motivated by a broader spectrum of grievances and focused on a wider range of targets than in the early post-9/11 period. In some cases, terrorist suspects appear to have sought a sense of organizational belonging, with little prejudice about which organization, as shown by the fact that they easily shifted allegiances between different groups. In others, an individual may have had a personal motivation but acted in the name of an FTO to aggrandize his or her own actions (or, in some cases, not acted in the name of an FTO at all). "Lone wolf" actors may turn out to have more in common with each other—regardless of motivation—than an HVE and an AFF have, for example. Focusing more on the motivation of actors—and resisting the temptation to label an attack as *terrorism* simply because the individual involved may have been Muslim or had a Middle Eastern background—could help us better understand, and therefore combat, the threat of terrorism in the United States.

---

[24] U.S. Federal Bureau of Investigation, *Terrorism 2002–2005*, Washington, D.C.: Federal Bureau of Investigation, undated.

[25] Jason Le Miere, "Why Isn't Las Vegas Shooting Being Called 'Terrorism' and Shooter Stephen Paddock a 'Terrorist'?" *Newsweek*, October 2, 2017; Scott Shane, "Terrorizing If Not Clearly Terrorist: What to Call the Las Vegas Attack?" *New York Times*, October 2, 2017.

[26] Masha Gessen, "Why We Should Resist Calling the Las Vegas Shooting 'Terrorism,'" *New Yorker*, October 3, 2017.

Individuals and Variables in the Terrorist Data Set

The data set developed for this report contains information about 476 individuals coded across approximately three dozen dimensions. These variables include biographical details on perpetrator demographics, terrorist activity history, and individuals' experience in the U.S. criminal justice system. Table A.1 defines each of these fields in more detail. As has been discussed in this report, it should be noted that in some cases, open-source information was not available, and thus not every variable could be coded for every individual included in the data set. Table A.2 identifies the 476 individuals examined in this report and contains codings of several key variables of interest.

Table A.1
Variables in the Terrorist Data Set

Variable Name	Description
case_number	Integer used as a unique identifier for every individual in the RAND data set.
first_name	Text field detailing terrorist's first name; in a handful of cases in which the suspect was a minor, this information is not publicly available.
middle_name	Text field detailing terrorist's middle name; in a handful of cases in which the suspect was a minor, this information is not publicly available.
last_name	Text field detailing terrorist's last name; in a handful of cases in which the suspect was a minor, this information is not publicly available.
alias	Text field identifying any known aliases used by the terrorist.
case_number/public_label	Alphanumeric code identifying the related court case number (e.g., 09-CR-10030) and/or the commonly used case or terrorist cell name (e.g., Boston Marathon Bombing or Lackawanna Six).
hometown	Text field identifying the town in which the perpetrator resided at the time of his or her arrest, death, or departure abroad. In some cases, this location may differ from the place where an act of terrorism was committed; in a few cases, the hometown is identified as a foreign location (e.g., Umar Farouk Abulmutallab, the "Christmas Day bomber," who was detained at Detroit Metropolitan Airport after failing to detonate a bomb on an international flight from Africa).
state	Text field corresponding to the hometown variable; in a few cases, this is a foreign country rather than a U.S. state.
gender	Text field indicating male or female.
age	Numeric field indicating the perpetrator's age at the time of his or her arrest, death, or departure abroad. In some cases, such as instances of U.S. citizens who traveled abroad and eventually died on the battlefield, these ages may differ (in which case we default to the older age as a coding rule).
role	Text field indicating at least one of six possible terrorist roles: (1) FF: A U.S. citizen or resident who successfully traveled abroad to join an FTO, namely in Afghanistan, Iraq, Libya, Syria, or Yemen (2) AFF: A U.S. citizen or resident who attempted to travel abroad to join an FTO but was arrested prior to boarding a plane or otherwise failed to reach his or her destination (3) HVE: An individual inside the United States who sought to conduct a terrorist attack domestically but who was not explicitly directed to do so by an FTO (4) DTO: An individual inside the United States who sought to conduct a terrorist attack domestically at the explicit direction of an FTO (5) Financier: An individual inside the United States who raised money on behalf of a terrorist organization (6) Facilitator: An individual inside the United States who provided nonmonetary material support to a terrorist organization (e.g., propaganda or equipment), or who helped recruit others to travel abroad to join an FTO, including providing them material support to travel

Table A.1—Continued

Variable Name	Description
status	Text field identifying whether the perpetrator was either arrested by law enforcement; remained at large either domestically or abroad (as of December 2016); or had been killed either by law enforcement, during a suicide attack, or on a foreign battlefield.
incident_date	Alphanumeric field indicating the date (day, month, year) that the perpetrator was arrested, died, or traveled abroad (if still at large).
indictment_date	Alphanumeric field indicating the date (day, month, year) that the perpetrator was formally charged or indicted; this date may or may not be the same as the arrest date.
plea_date	Alphanumeric field indicating the date (day, month, year) that the perpetrator entered a formal plea (guilty or not guilty), if applicable.
sentence_date	Alphanumeric field indicating the date (day, month, year) that the perpetrator was sentenced, if applicable.
judicial_district	Text field detailing the federal judicial district in which the individual was indicted and tried, if applicable.
charge_description	Text field describing the criminal charges faced by the individual, if applicable (e.g., conspiracy to provide material support to an FTO).
charges	Alphanumeric field identifying the specific statute(s) of the U.S. Code under which the individual was charged, if applicable (e.g., 18 U.S.C., Section 2339).
conviction_charges	Alphanumeric field identifying the specific statute(s) of the U.S. Code under which the individual was convicted or plead guilty, if applicable (e.g., 18 U.S.C., Section 2339).
sentence	Alphanumeric field describing the jail sentence and/or probation period faced by the perpetrator if criminal proceedings had been concluded (as of December 2016).
plea	Text field indicating whether the perpetrator plead guilty or not guilty, if applicable.
lawyer	Text field identifying the defendant's lawyer(s), if known.
dob	Alphanumeric field indicating the perpetrator's date of birth (day, month, year), if known.
pob	Text field identifying the perpetrator's country of birth, if known.
ethnicity_race	Text field identifying the perpetrator's ethnicity and/or race, if known.
citizenship	Text field describing the perpetrator's citizenship status, if known; individuals were generally classified as falling into one of five categories: (1) U.S.-born American citizen (2) Foreign-born, U.S. naturalized citizen (3) Foreign citizen in the United States on LPR status (4) Foreign citizen in the United States on legal, temporary status (e.g., a student visa) (5) Foreign citizen in the United States illegally

Table A.1—Continued

Variable Name	Description
convert	Text field identifying whether the perpetrator converted to Islam, if known.
education	Text field describing the perpetrator's highest level of education attained, if known; individuals were generally classified as falling into one of six categories: (1) Incomplete secondary-level education (2) High school graduation with no tertiary-level education (3) Some undergraduate-level education (4) Complete undergraduate-level degree (5) Some graduate-level education (6) Complete graduate-level degree
education_description	Text field noting schools attended and degrees completed by the perpetrator, if known.
group_association	Text field indicating FTO(s) to which the individual formally belonged or informally assisted, and/or with which the individual sympathized. In many cases, such as so-called lone wolves stimulated by electronic propaganda, the actual linkage between the individual and the FTO may be quite weak and/or inspirational in nature only.
fto_contact	Text field indicating whether the individual had any direct, known contact with an FTO; direct contact might include not only formal membership or training, but also electronic communication and the like.
mil_law_history	Text field noting whether the perpetrator had ever served in the military or for any law enforcement agency, if known.
criminal_history	Text field noting whether the perpetrator had ever been convicted of a crime (and if so, on what charges) before becoming radicalized and/or being indicted on terrorism charges or terrorism-related charges, if known.
mental_history	Text field noting whether the perpetrator was ever diagnosed with any mental illness, if known.
fbi_technique	Text field indicating any relevant law enforcement techniques used by the FBI or other agencies in order to identify and apprehend the perpetrator, including use of informants, confidential human sources, undercover agents/employees, or sting operations; tips received from a school, mosque, family member, friend, employer, or other member of the community; tracking of social media or other electronic footprints; discovery of inert explosive materials or indirect discovery during course of another investigation or random search; cooperation with foreign governments, militaries, and/or intelligence sources, including extradition proceedings and the like.
case_notes	Text field providing a brief narrative description of the case, including details about plots involved, radicalization process, groups involved, arrest/death history, and the like.

Table A.2
Individuals Contained in the Terrorist Data Set

First Name	Last Name	Year[a]	Hometown	State (or Country)	Gender	Age[a]	Status	Primary Role[b]	Primary Group Association[c]
Muhammed	Aatique	2003	Norristown	Pa.	Male	30	Arrested	FF	LeT
Akram	Abdallah	2008	Phoenix	Ariz.	Male	53	Arrested	Financier	Hamas
Rahmat	Abdhir	2007	San Jose	Calif.	Male	43	Arrested	Financier	JI
Nuradin	Abdi	2003	Columbus	Ohio	Male	32	Arrested	HVE	AQ
Zakaryia	Abdin	2017	Ladson	S.C.	Male	18	Arrested	AFF	ISIL
Naser	Abdo	2011	Fort Hood	Tex.	Male	21	Arrested	HVE	None ("jihad")
Abdow	Abdow	2009	Minneapolis	Minn.	Male	26	Arrested	Facilitator	al Shabaab
Abu	Abdul-Latif	2011	Tukwila	Wash.	Male	33	Arrested	HVE	None ("jihad")
Mohammad	Abdulazeez	2015	Hixson	Tenn.	Male	24	Killed (domestically)	HVE	None ("jihad")
Munir	Abdulkader	2015	West Chester	Ohio	Male	21	Arrested	HVE	ISIL
Agron	Abdullahu	2007	Buena Vista Township	N.J.	Male	24	Arrested	Facilitator	AQ
Mufid	Abdulqader	2004	Richardson	Tex.	Male	44	Arrested	Financier	Hamas
Hammad	Abdur-Raheem	2003	Falls Church	Va.	Male	34	Arrested	Facilitator	LeT
Zacharia	Abdurahman	2015	Columbia Heights	Minn.	Male	19	Arrested	AFF	ISIL
Bilal	Abood	2015	Mesquite	Tex.	Male	37	Arrested	FF	ISIL
Ahmad	Abousamra	2006	Mansfield	Mass.	Male	32	Killed (abroad)	FF	AQ
Patrick	Abraham	2006	Miami	Fla.	Male	26	Arrested	HVE	AQ

Table A.2—Continued

First Name	Last Name	Year[a]	Hometown	State (or Country)	Gender	Age[a]	Status	Primary Role[b]	Primary Group Association[c]
Khalid	Abshir	2009	Minneapolis	Minn.	Male	27	At large (abroad)	FF	al Shabaab
Ahmed	Abu Ali	2003	Falls Church	Va.	Male	22	Arrested	DTO	AQ
Hassan	Abu-Jihaad	2007	Phoenix	Ariz.	Male	31	Arrested	Facilitator	Taliban
Khalil	Abu-Rayyan	2015	Dearborn Heights	Mich.	Male	21	Arrested	HVE	ISIL
Mohammad	Abukhdair	2012	Mobile	Ala.	Male	25	Arrested	AFF	AQ
Umar	Abulmutallab	2009	Kaduna	Nigeria	Male	23	Arrested	DTO	AQAP
Moner	Abusalha	2013	Vero Beach	Fla.	Male	22	Killed (abroad)	FF	Jabhat al-Nusra
Dahir	Adan	2016	St. Cloud	Minn.	Male	22	Killed (domestically)	HVE	ISIL
Abdifatah	Aden	2013	Columbus	Ohio	Male	27	Killed (abroad)	FF	Jabhat al-Nusra
Muhammed	Afridi	2002	San Diego	Calif.	Male	28	Arrested	Facilitator	Taliban
Aref	Ahmed	2004	Niagara Falls	N.Y.	Male	27	Arrested	Financier	AQ
Farooque	Ahmed	2010	Ashburn	Va.	Male	34	Arrested	HVE	AQ
Hamza	Ahmed	2015	Minneapolis	Minn.	Male	19	Arrested	AFF	ISIL
Khaleel	Ahmed	2006	Chicago	Ill.	Male	25	Arrested	FF	None ("jihad")
Parveg	Ahmed	2017	Queens	N.Y.	Male	22	Arrested	AFF	ISIL
Salah	Ahmed	2009	Brooklyn Park	Minn.	Male	26	Arrested	FF	al Shabaab

Table A.2—Continued

First Name	Last Name	Year[a]	Hometown	State (or Country)	Gender	Age[a]	Status	Primary Role[b]	Primary Group Association[c]
Shirwa	Ahmed	2008	Minneapolis	Minn.	Male	26	Killed (abroad)	FF	al Shabaab
Syed	Ahmed	2006	Atlanta	Ga.	Male	21	Arrested	HVE	LeT
Zubair	Ahmed	2007	Chicago	Ill.	Male	28	Arrested	FF	None ("jihad")
Zarein	Ahmedzay	2010	Queens	N.Y.	Male	25	Arrested	HVE	AQ
Ali	Akhdar	2003	Dearborn	Mich.	Male	40	Arrested	Financier	Hezbollah
Elias	Akhdar	2003	Dearborn	Mich.	Male	31	Arrested	Financier	Hezbollah
Amera	Akl	2010	Toledo	Ohio	Female	37	Arrested	Financier	Hezbollah
Hor	Akl	2010	Toledo	Ohio	Male	37	Arrested	Financier	Hezbollah
Sami	Al-Arian	2003	Tampa	Fla.	Male	45	Arrested	Financier	PIJ
Anwar	Al-Awlaki	2011	Falls Church	Va.	Male	40	Killed (abroad)	FF	AQAP
Mukhtar	Al-Bakri	2002	Lackawanna	N.Y.	Male	21	Arrested	FF	AQ
Amin	Al-Baroudi	2015	Irvine	Calif.	Male	50	Arrested	Facilitator	Jabhat al-Nusra
Muhanad	Al-Farekh	2010	Winnipeg	Canada	Male	29	Arrested (abroad)	FF	AQ
Ibrahim	Al-Hamdi	2003	Alexandria	Va.	Male	25	Arrested	FF	LeT
Omar	Al-Hardan	2016	Houston	Tex.	Male	24	Arrested	AFF	ISIL
Aws Mohammed	Al-Jayab	2016	Sacramento	Calif.	Male	23	Arrested	AFF	Jabhat al-Nusra
Ali	Al-Marri	2011	Peoria	Ill.	Male	35	Arrested	DTO	AQ

Table A.2—Continued

First Name	Last Name	Year[a]	Hometown	State (or Country)	Gender	Age[a]	Status	Primary Role[b]	Primary Group Association[c]
Habis	Al-Saoub	2002	Portland	Oreg.	Male	37	Killed (abroad)	FF	Taliban
Ali	Al-Timimi	2003	Fairfax	Va.	Male	40	Arrested	Facilitator	LeT
Ahmed	Al-Uqaily	2004	Nashville	Tenn.	Male	33	Arrested	HVE	None ("jihad")
Abdurahman	Alamoudi	2003	Falls Church	Va.	Male	51	Arrested	Financier	AQ
Khalid	Aldawsari	2011	Lubbock	Tex.	Male	20	Arrested	HVE	None ("jihad")
Laith	Alebbini	2017	Dayton	Ohio	Male	26	Arrested	AFF	ISIL
Mohamed	Alessa	2010	North Bergen	N.J.	Male	20	Arrested	AFF	al Shabaab
Amer	Alhaggagi	2016	Oakland	Calif.	Male	21	Arrested	HVE	ISIL
Adarus	Ali	2009	Columbia Heights	Minn.	Male	25	Arrested	FF facilitator	al Shabaab
Amina	Ali	2010	Rochester	Minn.	Female	33	Arrested	Financier	al Shabaab
Ilyas	Ali	2002	San Diego	Calif.	Male	55	Arrested	Facilitator	Taliban
Abdul Raheem	Ali-Skelton	2016	Dearborn Heights	Mich.	Male	23	Arrested	HVE	ISIL
Sajmir	Alimehmeti	2016	Bronx	N.Y.	Male	22	Arrested	AFF	ISIL
Carlos	Almonte	2010	Elmwood Park	N.J.	Male	24	Arrested	AFF	al Shabaab
Yehia	Alomari	2008	Rochester	N.Y.	Male	26	Arrested	Financier	Hezbollah
Sahim	Alwan	2002	Lackawanna	N.Y.	Male	26	Arrested	FF	AQ
Waad	Alwan	2011	Bowling Green	Ky.	Male	30	Arrested	Facilitator	AQI
Mohammad	Amawi	2006	Toledo	Ohio	Male	26	Arrested	AFF	None ("jihad")

Table A.2—Continued

First Name	Last Name	Year[a]	Hometown	State (or Country)	Gender	Age[a]	Status	Primary Role[b]	Primary Group Association[c]
Ali	Amin	2015	Manassas	Va.	Male	17	Arrested	Facilitator	ISIL
Ryan	Anderson	2004	Fort Lewis	Wash.	Male	26	Arrested	Facilitator	AQ
Manssor	Arbabsiar	2011	Austin	Tex.	Male	56	Arrested	DTO	Iranian Quds Forces
Edward	Archer	2016	Yeadon	Pa.	Male	30	Arrested	HVE	ISIL
Yassin	Aref	2004	Albany	N.Y.	Male	34	Arrested	HVE	JeM
Enaam	Arnaout	2002	Chicago	Ill.	Male	41	Arrested	Financier	AQ
Abdul	Artan	2016	Columbus	Ohio	Male	18	Killed (domestically)	HVE	ISIL
Abdelhaleem	Ashqar	2004	Chicago	Ill.	Male	46	Arrested	Financier	Hamas
Burson	Augustine	2006	Miami	Fla.	Male	21	Arrested	HVE	AQ
Rothschild	Augustine	2006	Miami	Fla.	Male	22	Arrested	HVE	AQ
Khalid	Awan	2006	Brooklyn	N.Y.	Male	44	Arrested	Financier	KCF
Salim	Awde	2003	Dearborn	Mich.	Male	45	Arrested	Financier	Hezbollah
Jalil	Aziz	2015	Harrisburg	Pa.	Male	19	Arrested	FF facilitator	ISIL
Mohammed	Babar	2004	Queens	N.Y.	Male	31	Arrested	Facilitator	AQ
Muhanad	Badawi	2015	Anaheim	Calif.	Male	24	Arrested	Facilitator	ISIL
Shukri	Baker	2004	Garland	Tex.	Male	45	Arrested	Financier	Hamas
Michelle	Bastian	2016	Florence	Ariz.	Female	49	Arrested	Facilitator	ISIL
Thomas	Bastian	2016	Florence	Ariz.	Male	39	Arrested	HVE	ISIL

Table A.2—Continued

First Name	Last Name	Year[a]	Hometown	State (or Country)	Gender	Age[a]	Status	Primary Role[b]	Primary Group Association[c]
Narseal	Batiste	2006	Miami	Fla.	Male	32	Arrested	HVE	AQ
Jeffrey	Battle	2002	Portland	Oreg.	Male	31	Arrested	AFF	AQ
Craig	Baxam	2011	Laurel	Md.	Male	24	Arrested	AFF	al Shabaab
Emerson	Begolly	2011	New Bethlehem	Pa.	Male	21	Arrested	Facilitator	None ("jihad")
Shelton	Bell	2013	Jacksonville	Fla.	Male	19	Arrested	AFF	AQAP
Sabri	Benkhala	2003	Falls Church	Va.	Male	27	Arrested	FF	LeT
Mohimanul	Bhuiya	2014	Brooklyn	N.Y.	Male	25	Arrested	FF	ISIL
Soliman	Biheiri	2003	Herndon	Va.	Male	51	Arrested	Financier	Hamas
Ahmed	Bilal	2002	Portland	Oreg.	Male	24	Arrested	AFF	Taliban
Muhammad	Bilal	2002	Portland	Oreg.	Male	22	Arrested	AFF	Taliban
Carlos	Bledsoe	2009	Little Rock	Ark.	Male	23	Arrested	HVE	AQAP
John	Booker, Jr.	2015	Topeka	Kan.	Male	20	Arrested	HVE	ISIL
Daniel	Boyd	2009	Willow Spring	N.C.	Male	39	Arrested	HVE	HIG
Dylan	Boyd	2009	Willow Spring	N.C.	Male	22	Arrested	HVE	None ("jihad")
Zakariya	Boyd	2009	Willow Spring	N.C.	Male	20	Arrested	HVE	None ("jihad")
Ariel	Bradley	2014	Hixson	Tenn.	Female	29	At large (abroad)	FF	ISIL
Mahmud	Brent	2005	Baltimore	Md.	Male	32	Arrested	FF	LeT
Joseph	Brice	2011	Clarkston	Wash.	Male	20	Arrested	HVE	None ("jihad")

Table A.2—Continued

First Name	Last Name	Year[a]	Hometown	State (or Country)	Gender	Age[a]	Status	Primary Role[b]	Primary Group Association[c]
Ali	Brown	2014	Seattle	Wash.	Male	29	Arrested	HVE	ISIL
Avin	Brown	2014	Raleigh	N.C.	Male	21	Arrested	AFF	ISIL
Barry	Bujol, Jr.	2010	Hempstead	Tex.	Male	29	Arrested	AFF	AQAP
Cedric	Carpenter	2004	New Orleans	La.	Male	31	Arrested	Facilitator	ASG
Ali	Chandia	2003	College Park	Md.	Male	26	Arrested	Facilitator	LeT
Seifullah	Chapman	2003	Alexandria	Va.	Male	31	Arrested	AFF	LeT
Umar	Chaudhry	2009	Alexandria	Va.	Male	25	Arrested	AFF	Taliban
Zachary	Chesser	2010	Florence	Colo.	Male	20	Arrested	AFF	al Shabaab
Dayne	Christian	2016	Lake Park	Fla.	Male	31	Arrested	AFF	ISIL
Alexander	Ciccolo	2015	Adams	Mass.	Male	23	Arrested	HVE	ISIL
Heather	Coffman	2014	Glen Allen	Va.	Female	29	Arrested	FF facilitator	ISIL
Santos	Colon, Jr.	2015	Camden County	N.J.	Male	15	Arrested	HVE	ISIL
Shannon	Conley	2014	Boulder	Colo.	Female	19	Arrested	AFF	ISIL
Christopher	Cornell	2015	Green Township	Ohio	Male	20	Arrested	HVE	ISIL
James	Cromite	2009	Newburgh	N.Y.	Male	44	Arrested	HVE	JeM
Joshua	Cummings	2017	Denver	Colo.	Male	37	Arrested	HVE	ISIL
Ali	Daher	2003	Dearborn	Mich.	Male	41	Arrested	Financier	Hezbollah
Mohamad	Daher	2003	Dearborn	Mich.	Male	33	Arrested	Financier	Hezbollah
Muhammad	Dakhlalla	2015	Starkville	Miss.	Male	22	Arrested	AFF	ISIL

Table A.2—Continued

First Name	Last Name	Year[a]	Hometown	State (or Country)	Gender	Age[a]	Status	Primary Role[b]	Primary Group Association[c]
Adam	Dandach	2014	Orange	Calif.	Male	20	Arrested	AFF	ISIL
Aaron	Daniels	2016	Columbus	Ohio	Male	20	Arrested	AFF	ISIL
Adel	Daoud	2012	Chicago	Ill.	Male	18	Arrested	HVE	AQAP
Nelash	Das	2016	Landover Hills	Md.	Male	24	Arrested	HVE	ISIL
Abdirahman	Daud	2015	Minneapolis	Minn.	Male	21	Arrested	AFF	ISIL
Leon	Davis III	2014	Atlanta	Ga.	Male	37	Arrested	AFF	ISIL
Russell	Defreitas	2007	Brooklyn	N.Y.	Male	63	Arrested	HVE	AQ
Ralph	Deleon	2012	Ontario	Calif.	Male	23	Arrested	AFF	AQ
Kamal	Derwish	2002	Lackawanna	N.Y.	Male	29	Killed (abroad)	FF	AQ
Hinda	Dhirane	2014	Kent	Wash.	Female	46	Arrested	Financier	al Shabaab
Miguel	Diaz	2015	Miami	Fla.	Male	45	Arrested	HVE	ISIL
Issa	Doreh	2010	San Diego	Calif.	Male	54	Arrested	Financier	al Shabaab
Dritan	Duka	2007	Cherry Hill	N.J.	Male	28	Arrested	HVE	AQ
Eljvir	Duka	2007	Cherry Hill	N.J.	Male	23	Arrested	HVE	AQ
Shain	Duka	2007	Cherry Hill	N.J.	Male	26	Arrested	HVE	AQ
Hasan	Edmonds	2015	Aurora	Ill.	Male	22	Arrested	AFF	ISIL
Jonas	Edmonds	2015	Aurora	Ill.	Male	30	Arrested	HVE	ISIL
Samer	El Debek	2017	Dearborn	Mich.	Male	37	Arrested	DTO	Hezbollah

Table A.2—Continued

First Name	Last Name	Year[a]	Hometown	State (or Country)	Gender	Age[a]	Status	Primary Role[b]	Primary Group Association[c]
Ahmed	El-Gammal	2015	Avondale	Ariz.	Male	42	Arrested	FF facilitator	ISIL
Wesam	El-Hanafi	2010	Brooklyn	N.Y.	Male	33	Arrested (abroad)	Facilitator	AQ
Marwan	El-Hindi	2006	Toledo	Ohio	Male	43	Arrested	AFF	None ("jihad")
Amine	El-Khalifi	2012	Alexandria	Va.	Male	29	Arrested	HVE	AQ
Mohammad	El-Mezain	2004	San Diego	Calif.	Male	50	Arrested	Financier	Hamas
Hamze	El-Najjar	2009	Brooklyn	N.Y.	Male	27	Arrested	Financier	Hezbollah
Adnan	El-Shukrijumah	2014	Miramar	Fla.	Male	27	Killed (abroad)	FF	AQ
Basman	Elashi	2002	Richardson	Tex.	Male	46	Arrested	Financier	Hamas
Bayan	Elashi	2002	Richardson	Tex.	Male	47	Arrested	Financier	Hamas
Ghassan	Elashi	2002	Richardson	Tex.	Male	48	Arrested	Financier	Hamas
Hazim	Elashi	2002	Richardson	Tex.	Male	41	Arrested	Financier	Hamas
Ihsan	Elashi	2002	Richardson	Tex.	Male	42	Arrested	Financier	Hamas
Jaber	Elbaneh	2001	Lackawanna	N.Y.	Male	36	Arrested (abroad)	FF	AQ
Abad	Elfgeeh	2003	Brooklyn	N.Y.	Male	49	Arrested	Financier	AQ
Aref	Elfgeeh	2003	Brooklyn	N.Y.	Male	Unknown	Arrested	Financier	AQ
Mufid	Elfgeeh	2014	Rochester	N.Y.	Male	30	Arrested	FF facilitator	ISIL
Mahmoud	Elhassan	2016	Woodbridge	Va.	Male	26	Arrested	AFF	ISIL
Nader	Elhuzayel	2015	Anaheim	Calif.	Male	24	Arrested	AFF	ISIL

Table A.2—Continued

First Name	Last Name	Year[a]	Hometown	State (or Country)	Gender	Age[a]	Status	Primary Role[b]	Primary Group Association[c]
James	Elshafay	2004	Rossville	N.Y.	Male	19	Arrested	HVE	None ("jihad")
Mohamed	Elshinawy	2015	Edgewood	Md.	Male	30	Arrested	HVE	ISIL
Cabdulaahi	Faarax	2009	Minneapolis	Minn.	Male	32	At large (abroad)	FF	al Shabaab
Adnan	Farah	2015	Minneapolis	Minn.	Male	19	Arrested	AFF	ISIL
Mohamed	Farah	2015	Minneapolis	Minn.	Male	21	Arrested	AFF	ISIL
Unnamed minor (Colo. #2)	Farah	2014	Aurora	Colo.	Female	15	Arrested	AFF	ISIL
Unnamed minor (Colo. #3)	Farah	2014	Aurora	Colo.	Female	17	Arrested	AFF	ISIL
Abdulrahman	Farhane	2006	New York	N.Y.	Male	52	Arrested	Financier	AQ
Lyman	Faris	2003	Columbus	Ohio	Male	34	Arrested	DTO	AQ
Hatem	Fariz	2003	Spring Hill	Ill.	Male	30	Arrested	Financier	PIJ
Syed	Farook	2015	San Bernardino	Calif.	Male	28	Killed (domestically)	HVE	ISIL
Ahmed	Farouq	2015	Unknown	Unknown	Male	Unknown	Killed (abroad)	FF	AQAP
Joseph	Farrokh	2016	Woodbridge	Va.	Male	28	Arrested	AFF	ISIL
El Mehdi	Fathi	2014	Bridgeport	Conn.	Male	26	Arrested	HVE	None ("jihad")
Issam	Fawaz	2003	Dearborn	Mich.	Male	35	Arrested	Financier	Hezbollah
Rezwan	Ferdaus	2011	Ashland	Va.	Male	26	Arrested	HVE	AQ

Table A.2—Continued

First Name	Last Name	Year[a]	Hometown	State (or Country)	Gender	Age[a]	Status	Primary Role[b]	Primary Group Association[c]
Ahmed	Ferhani	2011	Queens	N.Y.	Male	26	Arrested	HVE	None ("jihad")
Michael	Finton	2009	Decatur	Ill.	Male	29	Arrested	HVE	AQ
Patrice	Ford	2002	Portland	Oreg.	Male	31	Arrested	AFF	AQ
Daniel	Franey	2016	Montesano	Wash.	Male	33	Arrested	HVE	ISIL
Adam	Gadahn	2015	Santa Ana	Calif.	Male	26	Killed (abroad)	FF	AQ
Faysal	Galab	2002	Lackawanna	N.Y.	Male	25	Arrested	FF	AQ
Sixto	Garcia	2015	Houston	Tex.	Male	20	Killed (abroad)	FF	ISIL
Yahya	Goba	2002	Bronx	N.Y.	Male	25	Arrested	FF	AQ
Arifeen	Gojali	2012	Riverside	Calif.	Male	21	Arrested	AFF	AQ
Joshua	Goldberg	2015	Orange Park	Fla.	Male	20	Arrested	Facilitator	ISIL
Ronald	Grecula	2005	Bangor	Pa.	Male	68	Arrested	Facilitator	AQ
Sebastian	Gregerson	2016	Detroit	Mich.	Male	29	Arrested	Facilitator	ISIL
Dahir	Guled	2010	Columbus	Ohio	Male	35	Killed (abroad)	FF	al Shabaab
Abror	Habibov	2015	Brooklyn	N.Y.	Male	30	Arrested	FF facilitator	ISIL
Hesham	Hadayet	2002	Irvine	Calif.	Male	41	Killed (domestically)	DTO	IG
Sulejmah	Hadzovic	2009	Brooklyn	N.Y.	Male	19	Arrested	AFF	AQ
Joshua	Haften	2015	Madison	Wisc.	Male	34	Arrested	AFF	ISIL

Table A.2—Continued

First Name	Last Name	Year[a]	Hometown	State (or Country)	Gender	Age[a]	Status	Primary Role[b]	Primary Group Association[c]
Mohammad	Hamdan	2014	Dearborn	Mich.	Male	22	Arrested	AFF	Hezbollah
Moussa	Hamdan	2009	Brooklyn	N.Y.	Male	37	Arrested	Financier	Hezbollah
Mohanad	Hammadi	2011	Bowling Green	Ky.	Male	23	Arrested	Facilitator	AQI
Omar	Hammami	2013	Daphne	Ala.	Male	25	Killed (abroad)	Facilitator	al Shabaab
Samy	Hamzeh	2016	Milwaukee	Wisc.	Male	23	Arrested	HVE	None ("jihad")
Armin	Harcevic	2015	St. Louis	Mo.	Male	37	Arrested	Financier	ISIL
Eric	Harroun	2013	Phoenix	Ariz.	Male	30	Arrested	FF	Jabhat al-Nusra
Khwaja	Hasan	2003	Fairfax	Va.	Male	27	Arrested	FF	LeT
Nidal	Hasan	2009	Fort Hood	Tex.	Male	38	Arrested	HVE	AQ
Sabirhan	Hasanoff	2010	Brooklyn	N.Y.	Male	34	Arrested (abroad)	Facilitator	AQ
Agron	Hasbajrami	2011	Queens	N.Y.	Male	27	Arrested	AFF	TTP
Syed	Hashmi	2006	New York	N.Y.	Male	26	Arrested	Facilitator	AQ
Burhan	Hassan	2009	Minneapolis	Minn.	Male	17	Killed (abroad)	FF	al Shabaab
Hawo	Hassan	2010	Rochester	Minn.	Female	63	Arrested	Financier	al Shabaab
Kamal	Hassan	2009	Minneapolis	Minn.	Male	24	Arrested	FF	al Shabaab
Mohamed	Hassan	2010	Minneapolis	Minn.	Male	22	At large (abroad)	FF	al Shabaab
Mohammad	Hassan	2009	Raleigh	N.C.	Male	22	Arrested	HVE	None ("jihad")

Table A.2—Continued

First Name	Last Name	Year[a]	Hometown	State (or Country)	Gender	Age[a]	Status	Primary Role[b]	Primary Group Association[c]
Adham	Hassoun	2002	Broward County	Fla.	Male	40	Arrested	Facilitator	AQ
Sami	Hassoun	2010	Chicago	Ill.	Male	22	Arrested	HVE	None ("jihad")
Maher	Hawash	2003	Portland	Oreg.	Male	38	Arrested	AFF	Taliban
Hamid	Hayat	2005	Lodi	Calif.	Male	22	Arrested	HVE	AQ
Umer	Hayat	2005	Lodi	Calif.	Male	47	Arrested	Facilitator	AQ
Latif	Hazime	2009	Dearborn	Mich.	Male	29	Arrested	Financier	Hezbollah
David	Headley	2009	Chicago	Ill.	Male	49	Arrested	FF	LeT
Erick	Hendricks	2016	Charlotte	N.C.	Male	35	Arrested	HVE	ISIL
Alex	Hernandez	2016	Worchester	Mass.	Male	31	Arrested	HVE	ISIL
Robert	Hester, Jr.	2017	Columbia	Mo.	Male	25	Arrested	HVE	ISIL
Marlonn	Hicks	2016	Crown Point	Ind.	Male	30	Arrested	HVE	ISIL
Ramiz	Hodzic	2015	St. Louis	Mo.	Male	40	Arrested	Financier	ISIL
Sedina	Hodzic	2015	St. Louis	Mo.	Female	35	Arrested	Financier	ISIL
Mohammed	Hossain	2004	Albany	N.Y.	Male	49	Arrested	HVE	JeM
Gregory	Hubbard	2016	West Palm Beach	Fla.	Male	52	Arrested	AFF	ISIL
Abdi	Hussein	2010	Minneapolis	Minn.	Male	35	Arrested	Financier	al Shabaab
Amir	Ibrahim	2013	Pittsburgh	Pa.	Male	32	Killed (abroad)	FF	ISIL
Unnamed minor (Colo. #1)	Ibrahim	2014	Aurora	Colo.	Female	16	Arrested	AFF	ISIL

Table A.2—Continued

First Name	Last Name	Year[a]	Hometown	State (or Country)	Gender	Age[a]	Status	Primary Role[b]	Primary Group Association[c]
Nabil	Ismail	2003	Dearborn	Mich.	Male	36	Arrested	Financier	Hezbollah
Yusra	Ismail	2014	St. Paul	Minn.	Female	20	At large (abroad)	FF	ISIL
Abdifatah	Isse	2009	Minneapolis	Minn.	Male	25	Arrested	FF	al Shabaab
Abdiweli	Isse	2009	Minneapolis	Minn.	Male	26	At large (abroad)	FF	al Shabaab
Darren	Jackson	2016	West Palm Beach	Fla.	Male	50	Arrested	AFF	ISIL
Robert	Jackson	2016	Pensacola	Fla.	Male	31	Arrested	Facilitator	ISIL
Mohamed	Jalloh	2016	Sterling	Va.	Male	26	Arrested	HVE	ISIL
Muna	Jama	2014	Reston	Va.	Female	36	Arrested	Financier	al Shabaab
Yusuf	Jama	2014	Minneapolis	Minn.	Male	21	Killed (abroad)	FF	ISIL
Kevin	James	2005	Los Angeles	Calif.	Male	29	Arrested	HVE	JIS
Kifah	Jayyousi	2005	Detroit	Mich.	Male	40	Arrested	Facilitator	AQ
Shueyb	Jokhan	2002	Broward County	Fla.	Male	24	Arrested	HVE	AQ
Joseph	Jones	2017	Zion	Ill.	Male	35	Arrested	HVE	ISIL
Maalik	Jones	2015	Baltimore	Md.	Male	31	Arrested (abroad)	FF	al Shabaab
Akba	Jordan	2014	Raleigh	N.C.	Male	22	Arrested	AFF	ISIL
Abdurasul	Juraboev	2015	Brooklyn	N.Y.	Male	24	Arrested	AFF	ISIL

Table A.2—Continued

First Name	Last Name	Year[a]	Hometown	State (or Country)	Gender	Age[a]	Status	Primary Role[b]	Primary Group Association[c]
Sohiel	Kabir	2012	Pomona	Calif.	Male	34	Arrested (abroad)	FF	AQ
Justin	Kaliebe	2013	Babylon	N.Y.	Male	18	Arrested	AFF	AQAP
Maodo	Kane	2009	New York	N.Y.	Male	38	Arrested	Financier	Hezbollah
Ikaika	Kang	2017	Waipahu	Hawaii	Male	34	Arrested	Facilitator	ISIL
Abdul	Kareem	2015	Phoenix	Ariz.	Male	43	Arrested	HVE	ISIL
Dilkhayot	Kasmiov	2015	Brooklyn	N.Y.	Male	26	Arrested	FF facilitator	ISIL
Moustafa	Kassem	2009	New York	N.Y.	Male	29	Arrested	Financier	Hezbollah
Troy	Kastigar	2008	Minneapolis	Minn.	Male	28	Killed (abroad)	FF	al Shabaab
Betim	Kaziu	2009	New York	N.Y.	Male	21	Arrested	FF	al Shabaab
Mohammad	Khalid	2011	Ellicott City	Md.	Male	17	Arrested	Facilitator	None ("jihad")
Asher	Khan	2015	Spring	Tex.	Male	20	Arrested	AFF	ISIL
Hafiz	Khan	2011	Miami	Fla.	Male	76	Arrested	Financier	TTP
Mahin	Khan	2016	Tucson	Ariz.	Male	18	Arrested	HVE	ISIL
Majid	Khan	2003	Catonsville	Md.	Male	23	Arrested	DTO	AQ
Masoud	Khan	2003	Gaithersburg	Md.	Male	31	Arrested	FF	LeT
Mohammed	Khan	2014	Bolingbrook	Ill.	Male	19	Arrested	AFF	ISIL
Rahatul	Khan	2014	Round Rock	Tex.	Male	24	Arrested	FF facilitator	ISIL
Raja	Khan	2010	Chicago	Ill.	Male	57	Arrested	Financier	AQ

Table A.2—Continued

First Name	Last Name	Year[a]	Hometown	State (or Country)	Gender	Age[a]	Status	Primary Role[b]	Primary Group Association[c]
Reaz	Khan	2013	Portland	Oreg.	Male	48	Arrested	Financier	AQ
Samir	Khan	2009	Charlotte	N.C.	Male	24	Killed (abroad)	FF	AQAP
Waqar	Khan	2009	Alexandria	Va.	Male	22	Arrested (abroad)	AFF	Taliban
Dilshod	Khusanov	2017	Villa Park	Ill.	Male	31	Arrested	AFF facilitator	ISIL
Mohamad	Khweis	2016	Alexandria	Va.	Male	26	Arrested	FF	ISIL
Mohamad	Kodaimati	2015	San Diego	Calif.	Male	24	Arrested	FF	ISIL
Ulugbek	Kodirov	2011	Birmingham	Ala.	Male	22	Arrested	HVE	IMU
Ali	Kourani	2017	Bronx	N.Y.	Male	32	Arrested	DTO	Hezbollah
Mahmoud	Kourani	2003	Unknown	Mich.	Male	32	Arrested	Financier	Hezbollah
Fazliddin	Kurbanov	2013	Boise	Ida.	Male	30	Arrested	HVE	IMU
Yong	Kwon	2003	Fairfax	Va.	Male	27	Arrested	FF	LeT
Hemant	Lakhani	2003	Hendon	United Kingdom	Male	66	Arrested	Facilitator	AQ
Colleen	LaRose	2009	Philadelphia	Pa.	Female	46	Arrested	FF	None ("jihad")
Gregory	Lepsky	2017	Point Pleasant	N.J.	Male	20	Arrested	HVE	ISIL
October	Lewis	2002	Portland	Oreg.	Female	25	Arrested	Financier	Taliban
John	Lindh	2001	San Anselmo	Calif.	Male	20	Arrested (abroad)	FF	AQ
Matthew	Llaneza	2013	San Jose	Calif.	Male	28	Arrested	HVE	Taliban

Table A.2—Continued

First Name	Last Name	Year[a]	Hometown	State (or Country)	Gender	Age[a]	Status	Primary Role[b]	Primary Group Association[c]
Terry	Loewen	2013	Wichita	Kan.	Male	58	Arrested	HVE	AQAP
Emanuel	Lutchman	2015	Rochester	N.Y.	Male	25	Arrested	HVE	ISIL
Fadl	Maatouk	2004	Orange Park	Fla.	Male	40	Arrested	Financier	Hezbollah
Haitham	Maghawri	2004	Richardson	Tex.	Male	35	At large (abroad)	Financier	Hamas
Ahmed	Mahamud	2011	Westerville	Ohio	Male	24	Arrested	Financier	al Shabaab
Hassan	Makki	2003	Dearborn	Mich.	Male	38	Arrested	Financier	Hezbollah
Daniel	Maldonado	2007	Houston	Tex.	Male	27	Arrested (abroad)	FF	al Shabaab
Tashfeen	Malik	2015	San Bernardino	Calif.	Male	29	Killed (domestically)	HVE	ISIL
Sayed	Malike	2003	Brooklyn	N.Y.	Male	43	Arrested	HVE	None ("jihad")
Mohamed	Mamdough	2011	New York	N.Y.	Male	20	Arrested	HVE	None ("jihad")
Imran	Mandhai	2002	Broward County	Fla.	Male	19	Arrested	HVE	AQ
Nicole	Mansfield	2013	Flint	Mich.	Female	33	Killed (abroad)	FF	Jabhat al-Nusra
Enrique	Marquez, Jr.	2015	Riverside	Calif.	Male	24	Arrested	Facilitator	ISIL
Antonio	Martinez	2010	Baltimore	Md.	Male	21	Arrested	HVE	None ("jihad")
Zakaria	Maruf	2009	Minneapolis	Minn.	Male	30	At large (abroad)	FF	al Shabaab
Mohamad	Masfaka	2010	Detroit	Mich.	Male	47	Arrested	Financier	Hamas
Shaker	Masri	2010	Chicago	Ill.	Male	26	Arrested	AFF	al Shabaab

Table A.2—Continued

First Name	Last Name	Year[a]	Hometown	State (or Country)	Gender	Age[a]	Status	Primary Role[b]	Primary Group Association[c]
Omar	Mateen	2016	Fort Pierce	Fla.	Male	29	Killed (domestically)	HVE	ISIL
Wassim	Mazloum	2006	Toledo	Ohio	Male	25	Arrested	AFF	None ("jihad")
Douglas	McCain	2014	San Diego	Calif.	Male	33	Killed (abroad)	FF	ISIL
Robert	McCollum	2015	Sheffield Lake	Ohio	Male	38	Arrested	HVE	ISIL
Terrence	McNeil	2015	Akron	Ohio	Male	24	Arrested	Facilitator	ISIL
James	Medina	2016	Hollywood	Fla.	Male	40	Arrested	HVE	ISIL
Adis	Medunjanin	2010	Queens	N.Y.	Male	24	Arrested	HVE	AQ
Tarek	Mehanna	2009	Sudbury	Mass.	Male	27	Arrested	Facilitator	AQ
Yonathan	Melaku	2011	Alexandria	Va.	Male	22	Arrested	HVE	AQ
Ahmad	Minni	2009	Alexandria	Va.	Male	20	Arrested	AFF	Taliban
Adnan	Mirza	2006	Houston	Tex.	Male	29	Arrested	AFF	Taliban
Akram	Mishal	2004	Richardson	Tex.	Male	Unknown	At large (abroad)	Financier	Hamas
Michael	Mixon	2007	Ardsley	N.Y.	Male	53	Arrested	Financier	AQ
Saeed	Moalin	2010	San Diego	Calif.	Male	33	Arrested	Financier	al Shabaab
Sharif	Mobley	2010	Buena	N.J.	Male	26	Arrested (abroad)	FF	AQAP
Hanad	Mohallim	2014	St. Louis	Minn.	Male	18	Killed (abroad)	FF	ISIL
Ahmed	Mohamed	2007	Tampa	Fla.	Male	26	Arrested	HVE	None ("jihad")

Table A.2—Continued

First Name	Last Name	Year[a]	Hometown	State (or Country)	Gender	Age[a]	Status	Primary Role[b]	Primary Group Association[c]
Alaa	Mohamed	2009	Brooklyn	N.Y.	Male	43	Arrested	Financier	Hezbollah
Liban	Mohamed	2015	Fairfax	Va.	Male	29	Arrested (abroad)	FF	al Shabaab
Omer	Mohamed	2003	San Diego	Calif.	Male	43	Arrested	Financier	AQ
Faisal	Mohammad	2015	Santa Clara	Calif.	Male	18	Killed (domestically)	HVE	ISIL
Ibrahim	Mohammad	2015	Toledo	Ohio	Male	36	Arrested	Financier	AQAP
Jude	Mohammad	2009	Raleigh	N.C.	Male	20	Killed (abroad)	FF	AQ
Gufran	Mohammed	2013	Dammam	Saudi Arabia	Male	30	Arrested	Financier	al Shabaab
Abdirahman	Mohamud	2014	Columbus	Ohio	Male	23	Arrested	FF	Jabhat al-Nusra
Ahmed	Mohamud	2011	San Diego	Calif.	Male	35	Arrested	Financier	al Shabaab
Mohamed	Mohamud	2010	Corvallis	Oreg.	Male	19	Arrested	HVE	AQAP
Mohamed	Mohamud	2010	San Diego	Calif.	Male	38	Arrested	Financier	al Shabaab
Donald	Morgan	2014	Rowan County	N.C.	Male	44	Arrested	AFF	ISIL
Jesse	Morton	2011	New York	N.Y.	Male	33	Arrested	HVE	AQ
Shafal	Mosed	2002	Lackawanna	N.Y.	Male	23	Arrested	FF	AQ
Jehad	Mostafa	2009	San Diego	Calif.	Male	28	At large (abroad)	FF	al Shabaab
Zacharias	Moussaoui	2001	Norman	Okla.	Male	33	Arrested	DTO	AQ
Abdulhakim	Muhammad	2009	Little Rock	Ark.	Male	23	Arrested	HVE	AQAP

Table A.2—Continued

First Name	Last Name	Year[a]	Hometown	State (or Country)	Gender	Age[a]	Status	Primary Role[b]	Primary Group Association[c]
Jamshid	Muhtorov	2012	Aurora	Colo.	Male	35	Arrested	AFF	IJU
Abdirahmaan	Muhumed	2014	Minneapolis	Minn.	Male	29	Killed (abroad)	FF	ISIL
Walli	Mujahidh	2011	Los Angeles	Calif.	Male	32	Arrested	HVE	None ("jihad")
Fareed	Mumini	2015	Staten Island	N.Y.	Male	21	Arrested	HVE	ISIL
Akram	Musleh	2016	Brownsburg	Ind.	Male	18	Arrested	AFF	ISIL
Hanad	Musse	2015	Minneapolis	Minn.	Male	19	Arrested	AFF	ISIL
Hoda	Muthana	2014	Hoover	Ala.	Female	20	At large (abroad)	FF	ISIL
Quazi	Nafis	2012	Queens	N.Y.	Male	21	Arrested	DTO	AQ
Arafat	Nagi	2015	Lackawanna	N.Y.	Male	44	Arrested	AFF	ISIL
Mohamed	Naji	2016	Brooklyn	N.Y.	Male	37	Arrested	AFF	ISIL
Patrick	Nayyar	2009	New York	N.Y.	Male	45	Arrested	Financier	Hezbollah
Sinh	Nguyen	2013	Garden Grove	Calif.	Male	23	Arrested	FF	Jabhat al-Nusra
Reza	Niknejad	2015	Woodbridge	Va.	Male	18	At large (abroad)	FF	ISIL
Abdi	Nur	2014	Minneapolis	Minn.	Male	20	At large (abroad)	FF	ISIL
Proscovia	Nzabanita	2010	Bristow	Va.	Female	26	Arrested	FF facilitator	al Shabaab
Abdulraham	Odeh	2004	Patterson	N.J.	Male	44	Arrested	Financier	Hamas

Table A.2—Continued

First Name	Last Name	Year[a]	Hometown	State (or Country)	Gender	Age[a]	Status	Primary Role[b]	Primary Group Association[c]
Ahmed	Omar	2009	Minneapolis	Minn.	Male	27	At large (abroad)	FF	al Shabaab
Guled	Omar	2015	Minneapolis	Minn.	Male	20	Arrested	AFF	ISIL
Sami	Osmakac	2012	Pinellas Park	Fla.	Male	25	Arrested	HVE	AQ
Khalid	Ouazzani	2010	Kansas City	Mo.	Male	32	Arrested	Financier	AQ
José	Padilla	2002	Ft Lauderdale	Fla.	Male	32	Arrested	DTO	AQ
Uzair	Paracha	2003	New York	N.Y.	Male	23	Arrested	FF facilitator	AQ
Gregory	Patterson	2005	Los Angeles	Calif.	Male	21	Arrested	HVE	JIS
Christopher	Paul	2007	Columbus	Ohio	Male	43	Arrested	HVE	AQ
Jamie	Paulin-Ramirez	2009	Leadville	Colo.	Female	31	Arrested	AFF	None ("jihad")
Laguerre	Payen	2009	Newburgh	N.Y.	Male	27	Arrested	HVE	JeM
Abdullah	Pazara	2013	St. Louis	Mo.	Male	38	Killed (abroad)	FF	ISIL
Stanley	Phanor	2006	Miami	Fla.	Male	31	Arrested	HVE	AQ
Jose	Pimentel	2011	New York	N.Y.	Male	27	Arrested	HVE	AQ
Tairod	Pugh	2015	Neptune	N.J.	Male	47	Arrested	AFF	ISIL
Haris	Qamar	2016	Burke	Va.	Male	25	Arrested	HVE	ISIL
Raees	Qazi	2012	Oakland Park	Fla.	Male	20	Arrested	HVE	AQAP
Sheheryar	Qazi	2012	Oakland Park	Fla.	Male	30	Arrested	Facilitator	AQAP
Shiraz	Qazi	2006	Houston	Tex.	Male	25	Arrested	AFF	Taliban

Table A.2—Continued

First Name	Last Name	Year[a]	Hometown	State (or Country)	Gender	Age[a]	Status	Primary Role[b]	Primary Group Association[c]
Mohammad	Qureshi	2004	Lafayette	La.	Male	47	Arrested	Financier	AQ
Imran	Rabbani	2015	Brooklyn	N.Y.	Male	17	Arrested	Facilitator	ISIL
Nemr	Rahal	2005	Detroit	Mich.	Male	41	Arrested	Financier	Hezbollah
Rania	Rahal	2005	Detroit	Mich.	Female	24	Arrested	Financier	Hezbollah
Ahmad	Rahami	2016	Elizabeth	N.J.	Male	28	Arrested	HVE	None ("jihad")
Usaamah	Rahim	2015	Roslindale	Mass.	Male	26	Killed (domestically)	HVE	ISIL
Adam	Raishani	2017	Bronx	N.Y.	Male	30	Arrested	AFF	ISIL
Azizjon	Rakhmatov	2016	Brooklyn	N.Y.	Male	28	Arrested	FF facilitator	ISIL
Jasminka	Ramic	2015	Rockford	Ill.	Female	42	Arrested	Financier	ISIL
Tahawwur	Rana	2009	Chicago	Ill.	Male	48	Arrested	Facilitator	LeT
Imdad	Ranjha	2007	Glen Burnie	Md.	Male	32	Arrested	Financier	AQ
Saifullah	Ranjha	2007	Laurel	Md.	Male	43	Arrested	Financier	AQ
Lamont	Ransom	2004	New Orleans	La.	Male	31	Arrested	Facilitator	ASG
Richard	Reid	2001	London	United Kingdom	Male	26	Arrested	DTO	AQ
Michael	Reynolds	2005	Wilkes-Barre	Pa.	Male	47	Arrested	HVE	AQ
Erwin	Rios	2013	Fayetteville	N.C.	Male	19	Arrested	AFF	None ("jihad")
Mohamed	Roble	2015	Minneapolis	Minn.	Male	20	At large (abroad)	FF	ISIL
Nadia	Rockwood	2010	King Salmon	Alaska	Female	36	Arrested	Facilitator	None ("jihad")

Table A.2—Continued

First Name	Last Name	Year[a]	Hometown	State (or Country)	Gender	Age[a]	Status	Primary Role[b]	Primary Group Association[c]
Paul	Rockwood, Jr.	2010	King Salmon	Alaska	Male	35	Arrested	Facilitator	None ("jihad")
Nihad	Rosic	2015	Utica	N.Y.	Male	26	Arrested	AFF	ISIL
Nicholas	Rovinski	2015	Warwick	R.I.	Male	25	Arrested	HVE	ISIL
Randall	Royer	2003	Falls Church	Va.	Male	30	Arrested	FF	LeT
Alaa	Saadeh	2015	West New York	N.J.	Male	23	Arrested	AFF	ISIL
Nader	Saadeh	2015	Rutherford	N.J.	Male	20	Arrested	AFF	ISIL
Rafiq	Sabir	2005	Boca Raton	Fla.	Male	50	Arrested	Facilitator	AQ
Ethsanul	Sadequee	2006	Roswell	Ga.	Male	20	Arrested	HVE	LeT
Saleh	Saeed	2008	Rochester	N.Y.	Male	27	Arrested	Financier	Hezbollah
Mahamed	Said	2015	Minneapolis	Minn.	Male	20	Arrested	HVE	ISIL
Akhror	Saidakhmetov	2015	Brooklyn	N.Y.	Male	19	Arrested	AFF	ISIL
Muhamaad	Salah	2004	Chicago	Ill.	Male	51	Arrested	Financier	Hamas
Mustafa	Salat	2009	Minneapolis	Minn.	Male	20	At large (abroad)	FF	al Shabaab
Ali	Saleh	2015	Queens	N.Y.	Male	22	Arrested	AFF	ISIL
Munther	Saleh	2015	Queens	N.Y.	Male	20	Arrested	HVE	ISIL
Asif	Salim	2015	Overland Park	Kan.	Male	35	Arrested	Financier	AQAP
Sultane	Salim	2015	Columbus	Ohio	Male	40	Arrested	Financier	AQAP
Mediha	Salkicevic	2015	Schiller Park	Ill.	Female	34	Arrested	Financier	ISIL
Hammad	Samana	2005	Los Angeles	Calif.	Male	21	Arrested	HVE	JIS

Table A.2—Continued

First Name	Last Name	Year[a]	Hometown	State (or Country)	Gender	Age[a]	Status	Primary Role[b]	Primary Group Association[c]
Muhammed	Saqi	2007	Washington	D.C.	Male	Unknown	Arrested	Financier	AQ
Ahmed	Sattar	2002	Staten Island	N.Y.	Male	43	Arrested	Facilitator	IG
Edward	Schimenti	2017	Zion	Ill.	Male	35	Arrested	HVE	ISIL
Pirouz	Sedaghaty	2005	Ashland	Oreg.	Male	47	Arrested	Financier	Chechen Mujahideen
Syed	Shah	2002	San Diego	Calif.	Male	53	Arrested	Facilitator	Taliban
Tarik	Shah	2005	Bronx	N.Y.	Male	42	Arrested	Facilitator	AQ
Faisal	Shahzad	2010	Bridgeport	Conn.	Male	30	Arrested	HVE	TTP
Kamran	Shaikh	2004	Queens	N.Y.	Male	35	Arrested	Facilitator	None ("jihad")
Derrick	Shareef	2006	Rockford	Ill.	Male	22	Arrested	HVE	None ("jihad")
Abdel	Shehadeh	2010	Honolulu	Hawaii	Male	21	Arrested	AFF	Taliban
Basit	Sheikh	2013	Raleigh	N.C.	Male	29	Arrested	AFF	Jabhat al-Nusra
Hysen	Sherifi	2009	Raleigh	N.C.	Male	24	Arrested	HVE	None ("jihad")
Omar	Shishani	2002	Detroit	Mich.	Male	43	Arrested	Financier	AQ
Mohamad	Shnewer	2007	Cherry Hill	N.J.	Male	22	Arrested	HVE	AQ
Mohamed	Shorbagi	2006	Rome	Ga.	Male	42	Arrested	Financier	Hamas
Ruben	Shumpert	2006	Seattle	Wash.	Male	26	Killed (abroad)	FF	al Shabaab
Aafia	Siddiqui	2008	Boston	Mass.	Female	36	Arrested (abroad)	FF	AQ

Table A.2—Continued

First Name	Last Name	Year[a]	Hometown	State (or Country)	Gender	Age[a]	Status	Primary Role[b]	Primary Group Association[c]
Asia	Siddiqui	2015	Queens	N.Y.	Female	31	Arrested	HVE	ISIL
Elton	Simpson	2015	Phoenix	Ariz.	Male	30	Killed (domestically)	HVE	ISIL
Shahawar	Siraj	2004	Queens	N.Y.	Male	22	Arrested	HVE	None ("jihad")
Hosam	Smadi	2009	Dallas	Tex.	Male	19	Arrested	HVE	AQ
Nadir	Soofi	2015	Phoenix	Ariz.	Male	34	Killed (domestically)	HVE	ISIL
Lynne	Stewart	2002	Brooklyn	N.Y.	Female	62	Arrested	Facilitator	IG
Harlem	Suarez	2015	Stock Island	Fla.	Male	23	Arrested	HVE	ISIL
Anes	Subasic	2009	Holly Springs	N.C.	Male	33	Arrested	HVE	None ("jihad")
Justin	Sullivan	2015	Morganton	N.C.	Male	19	Arrested	HVE	ISIL
Donald	Surratt	2003	Suitland	Md.	Male	30	Arrested	AFF	LeT
Yasein	Taher	2002	Lackawanna	N.Y.	Male	24	Arrested	FF	AQ
Mohammed	Taheri-azar	2006	Carrboro	N.C.	Male	22	Arrested	HVE	AQ
Serdar	Tatar	2007	Philadelphia	Pa.	Male	23	Arrested	HVE	AQ
Nicholas	Teausant	2014	Acampo	Calif.	Male	20	Arrested	AFF	ISIL
Keonna	Thomas	2015	Philadelphia	Pa.	Female	30	Arrested	AFF	ISIL
Zale	Thompson	2014	New York	N.Y.	Male	32	Killed (domestically)	HVE	ISIL
Samuel	Topaz	2015	Fort Lee	N.J.	Male	21	Arrested	AFF	ISIL
Abdella	Tounisi	2013	Aurora	Ill.	Male	18	Arrested	AFF	Jabhat al-Nusra

Table A.2—Continued

First Name	Last Name	Year[a]	Hometown	State (or Country)	Gender	Age[a]	Status	Primary Role[b]	Primary Group Association[c]
Dzhokhar	Tsarnaev	2013	Cambridge	Mass.	Male	19	Arrested	HVE	None ("jihad")
Tamerlan	Tsarnaev	2013	Cambridge	Mass.	Male	26	Killed (domestically)	HVE	None ("jihad")
Earnest	Ujaama	2002	Seattle	Wash.	Male	36	Arrested	Facilitator	AQ
"H.M."	Unknown	2014	Minneapolis	Minn.	Male	Unknown	At large (abroad)	FF	ISIL
Unnamed minor (Calif. #1)	Unknown	2015	Unknown	Calif.	Male	Unknown	Arrested	HVE	ISIL
Unnamed minor (Pa. #1)	Unknown	2014	Unknown	Pa.	Unknown	Unknown	Arrested	Unknown	ISIL
Unnamed minor (S.C. #1)	Unknown	2015	York	S.C.	Male	16	Arrested	HVE	ISIL
Unnamed minor (Va. #1)	Unknown	2003	Fairfax County	Va.	Male	Unknown	Arrested	Facilitator	AQ
Unnamed minor (Va. #2)	Unknown	2015	Woodbridge	Va.	Unknown	Unknown	Arrested	FF facilitator	ISIL
Noelle	Velentzas	2015	Queens	N.Y.	Female	28	Arrested	HVE	ISIL
Miguel	Vidriales	2012	Upland	Calif.	Male	21	Arrested	AFF	AQ
Bryant	Vinas	2008	Patchogue	N.Y.	Male	26	Arrested	FF	AQ
Mark	Walker	2004	Laramie	Wyo.	Male	19	Arrested	AFF	AIAI
Abdirizak	Warsame	2015	Eagan	Minn.	Male	20	Arrested	AFF	ISIL
Mohammed	Warsame	2004	Minneapolis	Minn.	Male	31	Arrested	FF	AQ
Levar	Washington	2005	Los Angeles	Calif.	Male	25	Arrested	HVE	JIS

Table A.2—Continued

First Name	Last Name	Year[a]	Hometown	State (or Country)	Gender	Age[a]	Status	Primary Role[b]	Primary Group Association[c]
Yusuf	Wehelie	2016	Alexandria	Va.	Male	25	Arrested	AFF	ISIL
David	Williams	2009	Newburgh	N.Y.	Male	28	Arrested	HVE	JeM
Kobie	Williams	2006	Houston	Tex.	Male	33	Arrested	AFF	Taliban
Lionel	Williams	2016	Suffolk	Va.	Male	27	Arrested	HVE	ISIL
Onta	Williams	2009	Newburgh	N.Y.	Male	32	Arrested	HVE	JeM
Randy	Wilson, Jr.	2012	Mobile	Ala.	Male	25	Arrested	AFF	AQ
Michael	Wolfe	2014	Austin	Tex.	Male	24	Arrested	AFF	ISIL
David	Wright	2015	Everett	Mass.	Male	24	Arrested	HVE	ISIL
Ziyad	Yaghi	2009	Raleigh	N.C.	Male	21	Arrested	HVE	None ("jihad")
Safya	Yassin	2016	Buffalo	Mo.	Female	38	Arrested	Facilitator	ISIL
Aman	Yemer	2009	Alexandria	Va.	Male	18	Arrested	AFF	Taliban
Jaelyn	Young	2015	Starkville	Miss.	Female	20	Arrested	AFF	ISIL
Nicholas	Young	2016	Fairfax	Va.	Male	36	Arrested	Facilitator	ISIL
Awais	Younis	2010	Arlington	Va.	Male	26	Arrested	HVE	None ("jihad")
Mohammad	Younis	2010	New York	N.Y.	Male	44	Arrested	Financier	TTP
Mohammed	Yousry	2002	Queens	N.Y.	Male	46	Arrested	Facilitator	IG
Abdullahi	Yusuf	2014	Inver Grove Heights	Minn.	Male	18	Arrested	AFF	ISIL
Mohamud	Yusuf	2010	St. Louis	Mo.	Male	24	Arrested	Financier	al Shabaab
Nima	Yusuf	2010	San Diego	Calif.	Female	24	Arrested	Financier	al Shabaab

First Name	Last Name	Year[a]	Hometown	State (or Country)	Gender	Age[a]	Status	Primary Role[b]	Primary Group Association[c]
Akmal	Zakirov	2015	Brooklyn	N.Y.	Male	29	Arrested	FF facilitator	ISIL
Ramy	Zamzam	2009	Alexandria	Va.	Male	22	Arrested	AFF	Taliban
Amanullah	Zazi	2010	Aurora	Colo.	Male	25	Arrested	Facilitator	AQ
Mohammed	Zazi	2009	Aurora	Colo.	Male	53	Arrested	Facilitator	AQ
Najibullah	Zazi	2009	Aurora	Colo.	Male	24	Arrested	HVE	AQ
Marcos	Zea	2013	Brentwood	N.Y.	Male	25	Arrested	AFF	AQAP

NOTES: AIAI = Al-Ittihad al-Islami; AQ = al Qaeda (core); AQI = al Qaeda in Iraq; AQAP = al Qaeda in the Arabian Peninsula; ASG = Abu Sayyaf Group; HIG = Hezb-e-Islami Gulbuddin; IG = Islamic Group (aka al-Gamaa al-Islamiyya); IJU = Islamic Jihad Union; IMU = Islamic Movement of Uzbekistan; ISIL = Islamic State of Iraq and the Levant; JeM = Jaish-e-Mohammed; JI = Jemaah Islamiyah; JIS = Jamiyyat Ul-Islam Is-Saheeh; KCF = Khalistan Commando Force; LeT = Lashkar-e-Taiba; PIJ = Palestinian Islamic Jihad; TTP = Tehrik-e-Taliban Pakistan.

[a] The years and ages identified in this table generally correspond to the years and ages at which the individuals were arrested, killed domestically by law enforcement during an attack, or are first believed to have traveled abroad to join an FTO. However, in the case of some FFs killed abroad, the exact date of departure from the United States could not be determined; in these instances, the estimated date of death on a foreign battlefield is used instead.

[b] As has been noted, in several cases individuals might arguably have fit the definition of multiple roles, such as both an HVE and an AFF. In such instances, we have endeavored to code a "primary" role based on our evaluation of the individuals' most egregious alleged activities, particularly as identified in public court filings, including unsealed indictments, criminal complaints, affidavits, etc. For a more detailed discussion of these coding issues, see the discussion of our methodological approach in Chapter One. For a more detailed definition of these role categories, see Table A.1.

[c] As has been noted, in several cases individuals were alleged to have associations—formal or informal—with multiple FTOs. In such instances, we have endeavored to code a "primary" association based on our evaluation of the individuals' closest ties, strongest inspirational sources, and/or earliest direct FTO contact, particularly as identified in public court filings, including unsealed indictments, criminal complaints, affidavits, etc. For a more detailed discussion of these coding issues, see the discussion of our methodological approach in Chapter One.

References

Aaronson, Trevor, "The Informants: The FBI Has Built a Massive Network of Spies to Prevent Another Domestic Attack. But Are They Busting Terrorist Plots—Or Leading Them?" *Mother Jones*, September–October 2011. As of August 21, 2018:
https://www.motherjones.com/politics/2011/07/fbi-terrorist-informants/

Akhter, Faheem, "Education, Dialogue, and Deterrence: Tools for Counter Terrorism," *Sociology and Anthropology*, Vol. 4, No. 4, 2016, pp. 257–262.

Alexander, Audrey, "A Year After San Bernardino, the Number of Women Jihadis Is Growing," Lawfare, December 18, 2016. As of August 21, 2018:
https://www.lawfareblog.com/year-after-san-bernardino-number-women-jihadis-growing

Anti-Defamation League, "Criminal Proceedings: A Timeline of US Terror Cases, 2002–2014," undated.

———, "Homegrown Islamic Extremism in 2014," April 2015. As of September 18, 2018: https://www.adl.org/sites/default/files/documents/assets/pdf/combating-hate/homegrown-islamic-extremism-in-2014-the-rise-of-isis-and-sustained-online-recruitment.pdf

Benmelech, Efraim, and Claude Berrebi, "Human Capital and the Productivity of Suicide Bombers," *Journal of Economic Perspectives*, Vol. 21, No. 3, 2007, pp. 223–238.

Benmelech, Efraim, Claude Berrebi, and Esteban Klor, "Economic Conditions and the Quality of Suicide Terrorism," *Journal of Politics*, Vol. 74, No. 1, 2012, pp. 113–128.

Bergen, Peter, "Post-9/11 Jihadist Terrorism Cases Involving U.S. Citizens and Residents: An Overview," March 13, 2011. As of August 21, 2018:
http://peterbergen.com/post-911-jihadist-terrorism-cases-involving-u-s-citizens-and-residents-an-overview/

Bergen, Peter, Courtney Schuster, and David Sterman, *ISIS in the West: The New Faces of Extremism*, Washington, D.C.: New America, November 2015. As of August 21, 2018:
https://static.newamerica.org/attachments/11813-isis-in-the-west-2/ISP-ISIS-In-The-West-Final-Nov-16-Final.66241afa9ddd4ea2be7afba9ec0a69e0.pdf

Berger, J. M., "The Evolution of Terrorist Propaganda: The Paris Attack and Social Media," testimony before the House of Representatives Committee on Foreign Affairs, January 27, 2015.

Berrebi, Claude, "Evidence About the Link Between Education, Poverty, and Terrorism Among Palestinians," *Peace Economics, Peace Science, and Public Policy*, Vol. 13, No. 1, January 2007, pp. 1–36.

Bloom, Mia, "Constructing Expertise: Terrorist Recruitment and 'Talent Spotting' in the PIRA, Al Qaeda, and ISIS," *Studies in Conflict & Terrorism*, Vol. 40, No. 7, 2017, pp. 603–623.

Borum, Randy, "Understanding the Terrorist Mindset," *FBI Law Enforcement Bulletin*, Vol. 72, No. 7, July 2003, pp. 7–10.

Brockhoff, Sarah, Tim Krieger, and Daniel Meierrieks, "Great Expectations and Hard Times: The (Non-Trivial) Impact of Education on Domestic Terrorism," *Journal of Conflict Resolution*, Vol. 59, No. 7, 2015, pp. 1186–1215.

Bueno de Mesquita, Ethan, "The Quality of Terror," *American Journal of Political Science*, Vol. 49, No. 3, 2005, pp. 515–530.

Byman, Daniel, "Comparing Al Qaeda and ISIS: Different Goals, Different Targets," testimony before the Subcommittee on Counterterrorism and Intelligence of the House Committee on Homeland Security, April 29, 2015.

Byman, Daniel, and Christine Fair, "The Case for Calling Them Nitwits," *Atlantic*, July–August 2010. As of August 21, 2018:
https://www.theatlantic.com/magazine/archive/2010/07/the-case-for-calling-them-nitwits/308130/

Byman, Daniel, and Jennifer R. Williams, "ISIS vs. Al Qaeda: Jihadism's Global Civil War," Brookings Institution, February 24, 2015. As of August 21, 2018:
https://www.brookings.edu/articles/isis-vs-al-qaeda-jihadisms-global-civil-war/

Campbell, Alexia Fernandez, "Why ISIS Recruiting in America Reached Historic Levels," *Atlantic*, December 6, 2015. As of August 21, 2018:
https://www.theatlantic.com/politics/archive/2015/12/why-isis-recruiting-in-america-reached-historic
-levels/433560/

Center on Law and Security, *Terrorist Trial Report Card: September 11, 2001–September 11, 2011*, New York: Center on Law and Security, New York University School of Law, January 2010.

Clarke, Colin P., "The Terrorist Diaspora: After the Fall of the Caliphate," testimony before the House Homeland Security Committee Task Force on Denying Terrorists Entry into the United States, July 13, 2017.

Clarke, Colin P., and Steven Metz, "ISIS vs. Al Qaida: Battle of the Terrorist Brands," *National Interest*, August 16, 2016. As of August 21, 2018:
https://nationalinterest.org/blog/the-buzz/isis-vs-al-qaida-battle-the-terrorist-brands-17370

Corner, Emily, and Paul Gill, "Is There a Nexus Between Terrorist Involvement and Mental Health in the Age of the Islamic State?" *CTC Sentinel*, Vol. 10, No. 1, January 2017, pp. 1–10.

Corner, Emily, Paul Gill, and Oliver Mason, "Mental Health Disorders and the Terrorist: A Research Note Probing Selection Effects and Disorder Prevalence," *Studies in Conflict & Terrorism*, Vol. 39, No. 6, pp. 560–568.

Counter Extremism Project, "Terrorists and Extremists Database," webpage, undated. As of July 16, 2017:
https://www.counterextremism.com/extremists

Cronin, Audrey Kurth, "Cyber-Mobilization: The New *Levée en Masse*," *Parameters*, Vol. 36, No. 2, Summer 2006, pp. 77–87.

Dahl, Erik J., "The Plots that Failed: Intelligence Lessons Learned from Unsuccessful Terrorist Attacks Against the United States," *Studies in Conflict & Terrorism*, Vol. 34, No. 8, 2011, pp. 621–648.

Faiola, Anthony, and Souad Mehhennet, "What's Happening to Our Children?" *Washington Post*, February 11, 2017.

Gartenstein-Ross, Daveed, and Nathaniel Barr, "Extreme Makeover, Jihadist Edition: Al-Qaeda's Rebranding Campaign," War on the Rocks, September 3, 2015. As of August 21, 2018: https://warontherocks.com/2015/09/extreme-makeover-jihadist-edition-al-qaedas-rebranding -campaign/

Gessen, Masha, "Why We Should Resist Calling the Las Vegas Shooting 'Terrorism,'" New Yorker, October 3, 2017. As of August 21, 2018: https://www.newyorker.com/news/news-desk/why-we-should-resist-calling-the-las-vegas-shooting -terrorism

Gill, Paul, Lone-Actor Terrorists: A Behavioural Analysis, Abingdon, England: Routledge, 2015.

Gill, Paul, and Emily Corner, "There and Back Again: The Study of Mental Disorder and Terrorist Involvement," American Psychologist, Vol. 72, No. 3, 2017, pp. 231–241.

Graff, Garrett, The Threat Matrix: The FBI at War in the Age of Terror, New York: Little, Brown and Company, 2011.

Habeck, Mary, "Assessing the ISIS–al Qaeda Split," SITE Intelligence Group, June 27, 2014. As of August 21, 2018: http://news.siteintelgroup.com/blog/index.php/categories/jihad/entry/193-assessing-the-isis-al-qaeda -split-the-origins-of-the-dispute-1

Hasan, Mehdi, "What the Jihadists Who Bought 'Islam for Dummies' on Amazon Tell Us About Radicalisation," New Statesman, August 21, 2014. As of August 21, 2018: https://www.newstatesman.com/religion/2014/08/what-jihadists-who-bought-islam-dummies -amazon-tell-us-about-radicalisation

Hegghammer, Thomas, "The Rise of Muslim Foreign Fighters: Islam and the Globalization of Jihad," International Security, Vol. 35, No. 3, Winter 2010–2011, pp. 53–94.

———, "Should I Stay or Should I Go? Explaining Variation in Western Jihadists' Choice Between Domestic and Foreign Fighting," American Political Science Review, Vol. 107, No. 1, February 2013, pp. 1–15.

Heibner, Stefan, Peter Neumann, John Holland-McCowan, and Rajan Basra, Caliphate in Decline: An Estimate of Islamic State's Financial Fortunes, London: International Centre for the Study of Radicalisation and Political Violence, 2017.

Helmus, Todd C., "Why and How Some People Become Terrorists," in Paul K. Davis and Kim Cragin, eds., Social Science for Terrorism: Putting the Pieces Together, Santa Monica, Calif.: RAND Corporation, MG-849-OSD, 2009. As of August 21, 2018: https://www.rand.org/pubs/monographs/MG849.html

Hill, Stephen M., "Community Policing, Homeland Security, and the Somali Diaspora in Minnesota," Democracy and Security, Vol. 13, No. 3, July 17, 2017, pp. 246–266.

Hoffman, Bruce, "The Use of the Internet by Islamic Extremists," testimony before the House Permanent Select Committee on Intelligence, May 4, 2006.

Human Rights Watch, Illusion of Justice: Human Rights Abuses in US Terrorism Prosecutions, New York: Human Rights Watch, 2014. As of August 21, 2018: https://www.hrw.org/report/2014/07/21/illusion-justice/human-rights-abuses-us-terrorism -prosecutions

Investigative Project on Terrorism, "Court Cases Database," webpage, undated. As of July 16, 2017: http://www.investigativeproject.org/cases.php

Jacques, Karen, and Paul Taylor, "Myths and Realities of Female-Perpetrated Terrorism," *Law and Human Behavior*, Vol. 37, No. 1, 2013, pp. 35–44.

Jenkins, Brian Michael, *Stray Dogs and Virtual Armies: Radicalization and Recruitment to Jihadist Terrorism in the United States Since 9/11*, Santa Monica, Calif.: RAND Corporation, OP-343-RC, 2011. As of August 21, 2018:
https://www.rand.org/pubs/occasional_papers/OP343.html

———, *Inspiration, Not Infiltration: Jihadist Conspirators in the United States*, Santa Monica, Calif.: RAND Corporation, CT-447, December 2015. As of August 21, 2018:
https://www.rand.org/pubs/testimonies/CT447.html

———, "Could ISIS and Al Qaeda, Two Giants of Jihad, Unite?" Fox News, March 14, 2016. As of August 21, 2018:
http://www.foxnews.com/opinion/2016/03/14/brian-jenkins-could-isis-and-al-qaeda-two-giants-jihad-unite.html

———, *The Origins of America's Jihadists*, Santa Monica, Calif.: RAND Corporation, PE-251-RC, December 2017. As of August 21, 2018:
https://www.rand.org/pubs/perspectives/PE251.html

Jenkins, Brian Michael, and Colin P. Clarke, "In the Event of the Islamic State's Untimely Demise . . . ," *Foreign Policy*, May 11, 2016. As of August 21, 2018:
https://foreignpolicy.com/2016/05/11/islamic-state-iraq-syria-baghdadi-plan-b/

Jones, Seth G., *Waging Insurgent Warfare: Lessons from the Vietcong to the Islamic State*, New York: Oxford University Press, 2017.

Jones, Seth G., Andrew Liepman, and Nathan Chandler, *Counterterrorism and Counterinsurgency in Somalia: Assessing the Campaign Against Al Shaba'ab*, Santa Monica, Calif.: RAND Corporation, RR-1539, 2016.

Jones, Seth G., James Dobbins, Daniel Byman, Christopher Chivvis, Ben Connable, Jeffrey Martini, Eric Robinson, and Nathan Chandler, *Rolling Back the Islamic State*, Santa Monica, Calif.: RAND Corporation, RR-1912, 2017. As of August 21, 2018:
https://www.rand.org/pubs/research_reports/RR1912.html

Kaplan, Eben, "Terrorists and the Internet," Council on Foreign Relations, January 8, 2009. As of August 21, 2018:
https://www.cfr.org/backgrounder/terrorists-and-internet

King, Michael, and Donald Taylor, "The Radicalization of Homegrown Jihadists: A Review of Theoretical Models and Social Psychological Evidence," *Terrorism and Political Violence*, Vol. 23, No. 4, 2011, pp. 602–622.

Kreuger, Alan, "Education, Poverty, and Terrorism: Is There a Causal Connection?" *Journal of Economic Perspectives*, Vol. 17, No. 4, 2003, pp. 119–144.

Kurzman, Charles, *Muslim-American Involvement with Violent Extremism, 2018*. As of September 18, 2018: https://kurzman.unc.edu/files/2018/01/Kurzman_Muslim-American_Involvement_with_Violent_Extremism_2018_01_18.xls

———, *Muslim-American Involvement with Violent Extremism, 2016*, Durham, N.C.: Triangle Center on Terrorism and Homeland Security, 2016.

Le Miere, Jason, "Why Isn't Las Vegas Shooting Being Called 'Terrorism' and Shooter Stephen Paddock a 'Terrorist'?" *Newsweek*, October 2, 2017. As of August 21, 2018:
https://www.newsweek.com/las-vegas-shooting-terrorism-terrorist-675476

Lee, Alexander, "Who Becomes a Terrorist? Poverty, Education, and the Origins of Political Violence," *World Politics*, Vol. 63, No. 2, April 2011, pp. 203–245.

Lichtblau, Eric, "F.B.I. Steps Up Use of Stings in ISIS Cases," *New York Times*, June 7, 2016.

Maher, Heather, "How the FBI Helps Terrorists Succeed," *Atlantic*, February 26, 2013. As of August 21, 2018:
https://www.theatlantic.com/international/archive/2013/02/how-the-fbi-helps-terrorists-succeed/273537/

Medina Mora, Nicolas, and Mike Hayes, "The Big (Imaginary) Black Friday Bombing," BuzzFeed News, November 15, 2014. As of August 21, 2018:
https://www.buzzfeednews.com/article/nicolasmedinamora/did-the-fbi-transform-this-teenager-into-a-terrorist

Melnick, Meredith, "Why Are Terrorists So Often Young Men?" *Huffington Post*, April 23, 2013. As of August 21, 2018:
https://www.huffingtonpost.com/2013/04/23/terrorists-men-violent-biology-boston-marathon_n_3117206.html

Metz, Steven, "The Internet, New Media, and the Evolution of Insurgency," *Parameters*, Vol. 42, No. 3, Autumn 2012, pp. 80–90.

———, "Can the U.S. Counter Terrorism's Shift to Decentralized and Radicalized Violence? *World Politics Review*, July 29, 2016. As of August 21, 2018:
https://www.worldpoliticsreview.com/articles/19505/can-the-u-s-counter-terrorism-s-shift-to-decentralized-and-random-violence

Moghaddam, Fathali, "The Staircase to Terrorism: A Psychological Exploration," *American Psychologist*, Vol. 60, No. 2, 2005, pp. 161–169.

———, *From the Terrorists' Point of View: What They Experience and Why They Come to Destroy*, Westport, Conn.: Praeger Security International, 2006.

Mossaad, Nadwa, and James Lee, *U.S. Naturalizations: 2014*, Annual Flow Report, Washington, D.C.: U.S. Department of Homeland Security, April 2016. As of August 21, 2018:
https://www.dhs.gov/sites/default/files/publications/Naturalizations_2014.pdf

Mueller, John, ed., *Terrorism Since 9/11: The American Cases*, Washington, D.C.: Cato Institute, March 2016.

Mueller, John, and Mark G. Stewart, "The Terrorism Delusion: America's Overwrought Response to September 11," *International Security*, Vol. 37, No. 1, Summer 2012, pp. 81–110.

Mulligan, Scott E. *Radicalization Within the Somali-American Diaspora: Countering the Homegrown Terrorist Threat*, Monterey, Calif.: Naval Postgraduate School, December 2009.

National Consortium for the Study of Terrorism and Responses to Terrorism, "Global Terrorism Database," webpage, undated. As of February 20, 2018:
https://www.start.umd.edu/gtd

Neumann, Peter R., "Foreign Fighter Total in Syria/Iraq Now Exceeds 20,000; Surpasses Afghanistan Conflict in the 1980s," International Centre for the Study of Radicalisation and Political Violence, January 26, 2015. As of August 21, 2018:
https://icsr.info/2015/01/26/foreign-fighter-total-syriairaq-now-exceeds-20000-surpasses-afghanistan-conflict-1980s/

New America, "Terrorism in America After 9/11: Part II. Who Are the Terrorists?" undated. As of February 15, 2018:
https://www.newamerica.org/in-depth/terrorism-in-america/who-are-terrorists/

Noguchi, Yuki, "Tracking Terrorists Online," *Washington Post*, April 19, 2006. As of August 21, 2018:
http://www.washingtonpost.com/wp-dyn/content/discussion/2006/04/11/DI2006041100626.html
?noredirect=on

Norris, Jesse J., and Hanna Grol-Prokopczyk, "Estimating the Prevalence of Entrapment in Post-9/11 Terrorism Cases," *Journal of Criminal Law and Criminology*, Vol. 105, No. 3, 2015, pp. 609–678.

Pascarelli, Paige, "Ideology à la Carte: Why Lone Actor Terrorists Choose and Fuse Ideologies," Lawfare, October 2, 2016. As of August 21, 2018: https://www.lawfareblog.com/
ideology-%C3%A0-la-carte-why-lone-actor-terrorists-choose-and-fuse-ideologies

Penman, Maggie, and Shankar Vedantam, "The Psychology of Radicalization: How Terrorist Groups Attract Young Followers," National Public Radio, December 15, 2015. As of August 21, 2018:
https://www.npr.org/2015/12/15/459697926/the-psychology-of-radicalization-how-terrorist-groups
-attract-young-followers

Rasmussen, Nicholas J., "Current Terrorist Threat to the United States," hearing before the Senate Select Committee on Intelligence, February 12, 2015.

Richardson, Josh, "The Somali Diaspora: A Key Counterterrorism Ally," *CTC Sentinel*, Vol. 4, No. 7, July 1, 2011, pp. 12–14.

Sageman, Marc, *Understanding Terrorist Networks*, Philadelphia: University of Pennsylvania Press, 2004.

Sageman, Marc, "A Strategy for Fighting International Islamist Terrorists," *Annals of the American Academy of Political and Social Science*, Vol. 618, No. 1, 2008, pp. 223–231.

Schneier, Bruce, "Portrait of the Modern Terrorist as an Idiot," *Wired News*, June 14, 2007. As of September 16, 2018:
https://www.wired.com/2007/06/securitymatters-0614/

Shane, Scott, "Terrorizing If Not Clearly Terrorist: What to Call the Las Vegas Attack?" *New York Times*, October 2, 2017. As of August 21, 2018: https://www.nytimes.com/2017/10/02/us/politics
/terrorism-las-vegas-attack.html

Silber, Mitchell, and Arvin Bhatt, *Radicalization in the West: The Homegrown Threat*, New York: New York City Police Department, 2007.

Simcox, Robin, "'We Will Conquer Your Rome': A Study of Islamic Terror Plots in the West," Henry Jackson Society, September 29, 2015. As of August 21, 2018:
https://henryjacksonsociety.org/2015/09/29/we-will-conquer-your-rome-a-study-of-islamic-state
-terror-plots-in-the-west-2/

Simcox, Robin, and Emily Dyer, *Al-Qaeda in the United States: A Complete Analysis of Terrorism Offenses*, London: Henry Jackson Society, 2013. As of August 21, 2018:
https://henryjacksonsociety.org/wp-content/uploads/2013/02/Al-Qaeda-in-the-USAbridged-version
-LOWRES-Final.pdf

Simon, Caroline, "The FBI Is 'Manufacturing Terrorism Cases' on a Greater Scale than Ever Before," Business Insider, June 9, 2016. As of August 21, 2018:
https://www.businessinsider.com/fbi-is-manufacturing-terrorism-cases-2016-6

Soufan Group, *Foreign Fighters: An Updated Assessment of the Flow of Foreign Fighters into Syria and Iraq*, New York: Soufan Group, December 2015. As of August 21, 2018:
http://soufangroup.com/wp-content/uploads/2015/12/TSG_ForeignFightersUpdate_FINAL3.pdf

Southers, Erroll, and Justin Heinz, *Foreign Fighters: Terrorist Recruitment and Countering Violent Extremism (CVE) Programs in Minneapolis–St. Paul: A Qualitative Field Study*, Los Angeles: National Center of Excellence for Risk and Economic Analysis of Terrorism Events, April 2015.

Stern, Jessica, "Pakistan's Jihad Culture," *Foreign Affairs*, Vol. 79, No. 6, November–December 2000, pp. 115–126.

Taha, Yousef, "Memorandum: ISIS-Related Prosecutions in the United States Through July 29, 2015," Rochester: Federal Public Defender's Office for the Western District of New York, July 29, 2015.

Thyne, Clayton, "ABCs, 123s, and the Golden Rule: The Pacifying Effect of Education on Civil War, 1980–1999," *International Studies Quarterly*, Vol. 50, No. 4, 2006, pp. 733–754.

Transactional Records Access Clearinghouse, Syracuse University, "TRAC Reports on Terrorism," webpage, undated. As of July 16, 2017:
http://trac.syr.edu/tracreports/terrorism/

United States v. Abu Khalid Abdul-Latif (aka Joseph Anthony Davis) and Walli Mujahidh (aka Frederick Domingue, Jr.), U.S. District Court, Western District of Washington at Seattle, Case No. MJ11-292, amended complaint for violations, June 23, 2011.

United States v. Tarek Mehanna and Ahmad Abousamra, U.S. District Court of Massachusetts, Cr. No. 09-CR-10017-GAO.

U.S. Census Bureau, *Educational Attainment: Five Key Data Releases from the U.S. Census Bureau*, Washington, D.C.: U.S. Census Bureau, undated, a. As of October 6, 2017:
https://www.census.gov/newsroom/cspan/educ/educ_attain_slides.pdf

———, "State Population Tables: 2010–2016," webpage, undated, b. As of October 6, 2017:
https://www.census.gov/data/tables/2016/demo/popest/state-total.html

———, *2013 American Community Survey of Somalis 3-Yr Estimate*, Washington, D.C.: U.S. Census Bureau, 2013.

U.S. Citizenship and Immigration Services, "Naturalization Fact Sheet," updated May 19, 2017. As of October 3, 2017:
https://www.uscis.gov/news/fact-sheets/naturalization-fact-sheet

U.S. Department of Justice, *Hearing Before the Committee on Oversight and Government Reform, United States House of Representatives, Entitled "Seeking Justice for Victims of Palestinian Terrorism in Israel," February 2, 2016*, Washington, D.C.: U.S. Department of Justice, undated. As of July 16, 2017:
https://oversight.house.gov/wp-content/uploads/2016/02/DOJ-Palestinian-Terrorism-5.10.16.pdf

———, *The Accomplishments of the U.S. Department of Justice, 2001–2009*, Washington, D.C.: U.S. Department of Justice, March 8, 2010. As of August 21, 2018:
https://www.justice.gov/sites/default/files/opa/legacy/2010/03/08/doj-accomplishments.pdf

U.S. Department of State, "Foreign Terrorist Organizations," undated. As of July 17, 2017:
https://www.state.gov/j/ct/rls/other/des/123085.htm

U.S. Federal Bureau of Investigation, *Terrorism 2002–2005*, Washington, D.C.: Federal Bureau of Investigation, undated. As of August 21, 2018:
https://www.fbi.gov/stats-services/publications/terrorism-2002-2005

———, "Ten Years After: The FBI Since 9/11. Investigative Highlights: Major Terrorism Preventions, Disruptions, and Investigations," press release, Washington, D.C.: Federal Bureau of Investigation, 2011.

U.S. House of Representatives, Homeland Security Committee, "Terrorist Threat Snapshot: Homegrown Jihadist Cases Since 9/11," webpage, undated. As of July 16, 2017: https://homeland .house.gov/map/

———, *Final Report of the Task Force on Combating Terrorist and Foreign Fighter Travel*, Washington, D.C.: Homeland Security Committee, March 2015.

Venhaus, John M., *Why Youth Join al-Qaeda*, Special Report 236, Washington, D.C.: U.S. Institute of Peace, May 2010.

Vidino, Lorenzo, and Seamus Hughes, *ISIS in America: From Retweets to Raqqa*, Washington, D.C.: George Washington University Program on Extremism, December 2015.

Walters, Riley, "An Interactive Timeline of the 85 Islamist Terror Plots Since 9/11," *Daily Signal*, May 16, 2016.

Watts, Clint, "ISIS and al Qaeda Race to the Bottom: The Next Attacks," *Foreign Affairs*, November 23, 2015. As of August 21, 2018:
https://www.foreignaffairs.com/articles/2015-11-23/isis-and-al-qaeda-race-bottom

Weimann, Gabriel, *www.terror.net: How Modern Terrorism Uses the Internet*, Special Report 116, Washington, D.C.: U.S. Institute of Peace, March 2004.

———, *Terror on the Internet: The New Arena, the New* Challenges, Washington, D.C.: USIP Press Books, March 2006.

———, *New Terrorism and New Media*, Research Series, Vol. 2, Washington, D.C.: Woodrow Wilson International Center for Scholars, 2014.

Weine, Stevan, and Osman Ahmed, *Building Resilience to Violent Extremism Among Somali-Americans in Minneapolis–St. Paul*, College Park, Md.: National Consortium for the Study of Terrorism and Responses to Terrorism, 2012. As of August 21, 2018:
https://www.start.umd.edu/sites/default/files/files/publications/Weine_BuildingResiliencetoViolentE xtremism_SomaliAmericans.pdf

Wiktorowicz, Quitan, "Joining the Cause: Al-Muhajiroun and Radical Islam," paper presented at the Roots of Islamic Radicalism Conference, Yale University, 2004.

Winter, Charlie, *ICSR Insight: The ISIS Propaganda Decline*, London: International Centre for the Study of Radicalisation and Political Violence, March 23, 2017a.

———, "What I Learned from Reading the Islamic State's Propaganda Instruction Manual," Lawfare, April 2, 2017b. As of August 21, 2018:
https://www.lawfareblog.com/what-i-learned-reading-islamic-states-propaganda-instruction-manual

Winter, Charlie, and Jade Parker, "Virtual Caliphate Rebooted: The Islamic State's Evolving Online Strategy," Lawfare, January 7, 2018. As of August 21, 2018:
https://www.lawfareblog.com/virtual-caliphate-rebooted-islamic-states-evolving-online-strategy

Zabel, Richard, and James Benjamin, Jr., *In Pursuit of Justice: Prosecuting Terrorism Cases in the Federal Courts*, New York: Human Rights First, May 2008.

Zelin, Aaron, *ICSR Insight: Up to 11,000 Foreign Fighters in Syria, Steep Rise Among Western Europeans*, London: International Centre for the Study of Radicalisation and Political Violence, December 12, 2013.

Zuckerman, Jessica, Steven Bucci, and James Jay Carafano, "60 Terrorist Plots Since 9/11: Continued Lessons in Domestic Counterterrorism," Special Report #137 on Terrorism, Washington, D.C.: Heritage Foundation, July 22, 2013.